BIBLE CHARACTERS

VISUAL ENCYCLOPEDIA

DK

Penguin Random House

DK Delhi

Senior Editor Bharti Bedi
Project Art Editor Pooja Pipil
Editor Neha Ruth Samuel
Art Editors Sonali Rawat, Ravi Indiver
Assistant Art Editor Rohit Bhardwaj
Jacket Designer Tanya Mehrotra
Jackets Editorial Coordinator Priyanka Sharma
Senior DTP Designer Harish Aggarwal
DTP Designers Rajesh Singh Adhikari,
Syed Md Farhan, Sachin Gupta
Picture Researcher Nishwan Rasool
Managing Jackets Editor Saloni Singh
Picture Research Manager Taiyaba Khatoon
Pre-production Manager Balwant Singh
Production Manager Pankaj Sharma
Managing Editor Kingshuk Ghoshal
Managing Art Editor Govind Mittal

DK London

Editor Jessica Cawthra
Senior Art Editor Spencer Holbrook
Jacket Editor Claire Gell
Senior Jacket Designer Mark Cavanagh
Jacket Design Development Manager Sophia MTT
Producer, Pre-production Gillian Reid
Senior Producer Angela Graef
Managing Editor Francesca Baines
Managing Art Editor Philip Letsu
Publisher Andrew Macintyre
Art Director Karen Self
Associate Publishing Director Liz Wheeler
Design Director Philip Ormerod
Publishing Director Jonathan Metcalf

Written by Peter Chrisp
Consultant: Rev Dr Stephen Motyer
Illustrations by Peter Dennis

First published in Great Britain in 2018
by Dorling Kindersley Limited
80 Strand, London WC2R ORL

Copyright © 2018 Dorling Kindersley Limited

A Penguin Random House Company
10 9 8 7 6 5 4 3 2 1
001–307062–March/2018

A CIP catalogue record for this book is available
from the British Library.

ISBN 978-0-2413-0961-2

Printed in Hong Kong

Bible quotations from the Holy Bible, New International Version

A WORLD OF IDEAS:
SEE ALL THERE IS TO KNOW

www.dk.com

BIBLE CHARACTERS

VISUAL ENCYCLOPEDIA

CONTENTS

1

Abraham leads Isaac up the Mountains of Moriah.

Samuel hears God's call to become a prophet.

An angel tells the women that Jesus has risen from the dead.

3

Jesus clears the temple of the corrupt money changers.

BOOKS OF THE BIBLE

The Bible gets its name from the Greek word *biblia*, which means "books". This is because the Bible is made up of many different books. It is divided into two parts – the Jewish Bible, called the Old Testament by Christians, and the Christian New Testament. The Bible is the most widely read book in history. Its story of one, all-powerful God forms the basis of three religions – Judaism, Christianity, and Islam.

THE JEWISH BIBLE

Jews still read from scrolls in their synagogues (Jewish places of worship). The Torah scroll (left) is made up of the first five books of the Jewish Bible. The sacred Torah is still used in the traditional scroll form, adding to its special status.

THE NEW TESTAMENT

Early Christian writers wrote the New Testament, which is about the life of Jesus and his followers. In the 2nd century CE, Christians stopped using scrolls and began using a codex (book with pages). Shown below is the oldest surviving copy of a codex of the Gospel of John, from the late 2nd century CE.

DEAD SEA SCROLLS

The books of the Bible were originally written on scrolls. Scrolls, like the one above, were found in pottery jars by the Dead Sea, in 1947. These Dead Sea Scrolls, some dating back to the 2nd century BCE, reveal that there was no "fixed" Jewish Bible at the time the scrolls were written. Between 90 and 135 CE, Jewish rabbis (teachers) agreed upon a version of the Jewish Bible that continues to be used today.

WORKS OF ART

Throughout the Middle Ages, Bibles were copied by monks and decorated by hand. Some copies had ornate illustrations, and were the treasured possessions of monasteries, churches, and royal courts. This page (left), from the Lindisfarne Gospels, was made by monks in northern England in the 8th century CE.

ST JEROME

Originally written in Hebrew and Greek, the Bible has been translated into more than 2,000 languages. One of the most influential translations was the Latin one, made by St Jerome (above), a priest, who lived in the 4th century CE. The Lindisfarne Gospels were written using this translation.

PRINTING THE BIBLE

In the 1440s, a German publisher called Johannes Gutenberg invented the printing press, allowing many more people to read books. The first book he printed was a copy of St Jerome's Latin Bible (left). Since then, billions of Bibles have been printed. It carries on being the best-selling book ever.

THE COVENANTS OF THE BIBLE

The Bible tells the story of a series of covenants (binding agreements) made between God and people, based on promises given by God. The Old Testament talks of God's covenants with the Israelites, his chosen people, while in the New Testament, Jesus makes a new covenant with all of humanity. The word "testament" comes from the Latin *testamentum*, which itself has been translated from the Greek word for a formal agreement or will.

2. NOAH AND THE RAINBOW

Later, God sends a great flood to wipe out wicked humankind, sparing only Noah and his family. He promises Noah he will never send another flood like this, setting a rainbow in the sky as a sign of his covenant.

1. ADAM AND EVE

In the Bible, God makes a covenant with the first people – Adam and Eve. God places them in the Garden of Eden, giving them this perfect place to live, and immortality. This is only promised to them as long as they do not eat the fruit of the tree of knowledge of good and evil. But they disobey God and eat the fruit, becoming mortal and breaking the covenant.

4. MOSES AND THE LAW

After God rescues the Israelites from slavery in Egypt, he makes a new covenant with Moses. God says he has chosen the Israelites to be a holy nation, and he gives them new laws. The most important are the Ten Commandments, written on stone tablets, which he gives to Moses.

3. THE PROMISED LAND

God's next covenant is with Abraham. God promises Abraham he will be the father of a great nation. In return, Abraham must obey God's commands. As instructed, Abraham leaves his homeland for Canaan, a new land promised to his descendants by God.

5. KINGDOM OF ISRAEL

The Israelites break the covenant God made with Moses by not following the Law, and so God lets Israel's enemies defeat them. Then, God makes a new covenant with King David, telling him that if the Israelites follow the Law, then God promises that David's descendants will rule over the Kingdom of Israel. In this picture, David is shown bringing the Ark of the Covenant, holding the Ten Commandments, into Jerusalem.

6. THE NEW COVENANT

In the New Testament, God sends his son, Jesus, to make the final covenant with humankind. Jesus offers forgiveness for sins, and eternal life to all those who believe in him. This painting depicts the Last Supper, the final meal that Jesus shared with his followers before his death. Here, Jesus made the wine a symbol of "the new covenant in my blood".

NOAH'S ARK
This 13th-century mosaic, in St Mark's Basilica, Venice, shows the story of Noah's ark. In this scene, Noah is loading the ark with two of every living creature, to save them from the flood.

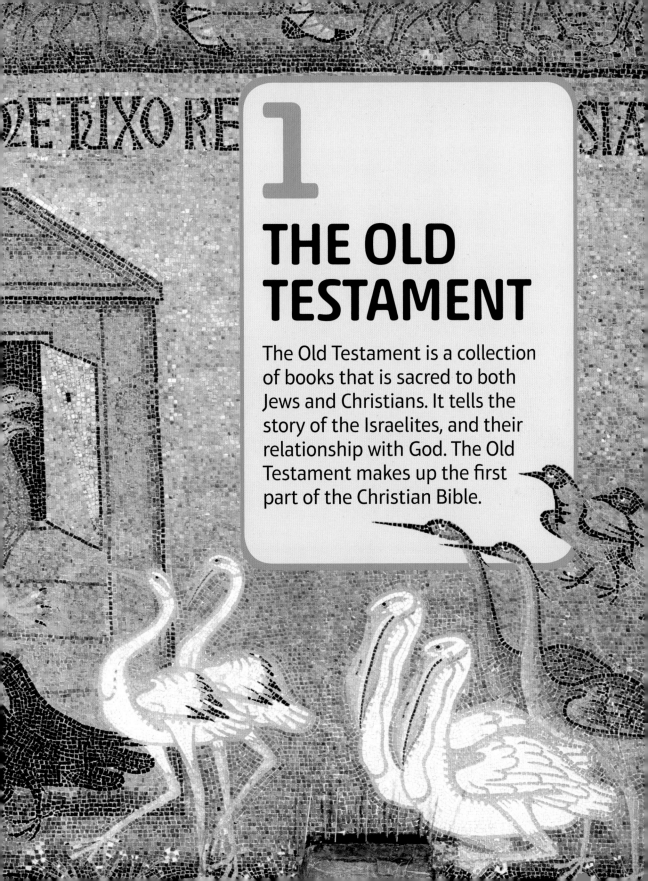

1
THE OLD TESTAMENT

The Old Testament is a collection of books that is sacred to both Jews and Christians. It tells the story of the Israelites, and their relationship with God. The Old Testament makes up the first part of the Christian Bible.

THE OLD TESTAMENT

The Old Testament is the Christian name for the holy book of the Jewish people, sacred also to Christians. Also known by Jews as the Tanakh, which is written in Hebrew, it tells the stories of the Israelites and their God. The Old Testament was mostly written down between the 8th and 3rd centuries BCE, though some parts of it are much older. It has three sections, but for Jews, the most important part is the Torah, which contains the Law of Moses.

THE PROPHETS

The section called Nevi'im contains the writings of Israelite prophets. The word "prophet" comes from a Greek word meaning someone who speaks for a god. Old Testament prophets, such as Elijah, were believed to speak on behalf of God, who took care of them. This picture shows Elijah in the wilderness, being fed by a raven sent by God.

THE TORAH

The Old Testament contains the same sacred books for Jews and Christians, though the order differs slightly. Jews divide it into three sections – the Torah (instruction), Nevi'im (prophets), and Kethubim (writings). The first letters of these three sections make up the name of the "Tanakh". The Torah is a set of five books written by Moses and the Torah scroll (above) is the most sacred object for Jewish people.

BOOK OF PSALMS

The Book of Psalms is the first book of the third section, Kethubim. It is a collection of songs praising God and expressing sorrow for the sufferings of the Israelites. Seventy-three of them are called "a Psalm of David". These may have been composed by King David, the great warrior king of Israel, who fought Goliath and captured Jerusalem. King David is shown on this ivory plaque.

EXPLAINING NUMBERS

In the Old Testament numbers are used in different ways. While some, such as the size of the tabernacle, the shrine of the Israelites (above), are accurate, other numbers are symbolic. For example, the "forty years" during which the Israelites live on manna (a type of bread), and the "forty days and forty nights" that Moses spends on Mount Sinai receiving the Ten Commandments, simply indicate a long period of time.

THE SIGNIFICANCE OF NAMES

Many Hebrew names of people in the Old Testament have religious meanings. This mosaic shows the prophet Daniel, whose name means "God is my judge". Other Old Testament names with meanings are Joshua ("God is Saviour"), Ezekiel ("God strengthens"), and Jeremiah ("God has lifted up").

JEWISH FESTIVALS

The stories of the Old Testament are remembered in many Jewish festivals. The most important is Passover, a festival held in spring, in memory of the Israelites' escape from slavery in Egypt. Jewish families celebrate Passover with a special meal.

ADAM AND EVE

Genesis, Chapter 2

After God made the earth, he made a man from the dust on the ground and breathed life into him. He called the man Adam. As a home for Adam, God planted a garden in Eden. In the middle stood the tree of life and the tree of the knowledge of good and evil. God told Adam that he could eat the fruit of any tree in the garden, apart from the tree of the knowledge of good and evil. If Adam ate the fruit of this tree, he would surely die. God then invited Adam to name all the animals and birds, setting humankind above all other living things.

The word "genesis" comes from the **Greek word for "beginning"**.

ADAM SLEEPS

Adam named all the animals in the garden, but he was still on his own. God worried that Adam would be lonely. So he made him fall into a deep sleep, opened his side, and drew out a rib. He used the rib to make a woman as a companion for Adam.

»

CHAPTER 2 VERSE 9

"... the tree of life..."

Adam and Eve may eat freely from the tree of life, which offers eternal life. As long as they obey God, they can live forever.

The tree of the knowledge of good and evil

ADAM'S WIFE

Adam and the woman faced each other for the first time in the Garden of Eden, and although they were naked, they felt no shame. The woman did not yet have a name, though Adam later called her Eve.

Eve

Adam

The Old Testament

God punished the snake by **making it crawl on its belly**.

The snake convinces Eve to eat the fruit of the tree of knowledge.

Adam eats the fruit.

EATING THE FRUIT

As soon as Adam and Eve ate the fruit, they realized that they were naked and felt ashamed. They made themselves coverings of fig leaves, and hid from God. When God asked them if they had eaten the fruit from the tree of knowledge, they could not deny it. Adam blamed Eve, and Eve blamed the snake.

TREE OF KNOWLEDGE
Genesis, Chapter 3

Of all the animals made by God, the most cunning was the snake. Seeing the woman, Eve, the snake asked her if God had told her not to eat any fruit in the garden. She told the snake that if she ate the fruit of the tree of knowledge of good and evil, she would die. The snake said that she would surely not die. He told her that if she ate this fruit, she would become wise, like God. So Eve ate the fruit, and also gave some to Adam. At once, they became aware of good and evil.

Adam and Eve are banished from the garden.

PUNISHED BY GOD

God punished Adam and Eve by taking away the gift of eternal life. To stop them from eating from the tree of life, he drove them out of the garden. God told Adam that he would have to work the ground from now on, while Eve would feel pain in childbirth.

CAIN AND ABEL

Genesis, Chapter 4

Abel keeps flocks of sheep.

Abel

Cain

TWO WAYS

The brothers followed different ways of making a living from the land. Cain settled in an area to farm the land and plant crops, while Abel kept sheep, and went from place to place, looking for fresh grazing.

Cain runs away from his crime.

Adam and Eve had two sons, the older called Cain and the younger called Abel. When they grew up, Abel became a shepherd, while Cain worked the land. Both brothers made offerings to God. While Cain offered some fruits of the soil, Abel chose the best portions of meat from his firstborn animals. God preferred Abel's offering, which had been chosen with care, to Cain's. Jealous of his brother, Cain asked Abel to go to a field with him. Here, Cain attacked Abel and killed him. For this act, God punished Cain with a curse, making him a restless wanderer on earth for the rest of his days.

CAIN DENIES HIS CRIME

Cain foolishly thought he could keep the murder a secret. When God asked him where his brother was, Cain replied that he did not know, and asked, "Am I my brother's keeper?" He showed no remorse for the crime.

The Old Testament

CHAPTER 4 VERSE 5

"... on Cain and his offering he did not look with favor."

The Bible does not explain why God rejects Cain's offering. The reason is probably because, under Israelite law, the firstborn animals and the first fruits harvested were offered to God. Cain's mistake is not offering his first fruits but just some of his harvest.

✥

CHAPTER 4 VERSE 15

" ... put a mark on Cain..."

The Bible does not say what kind of mark God put on Cain, but the mark is both a sign of Cain's sin and a symbol of God's protection.

In the Bible, **the word sin** is mentioned here **for the first time**.

CAIN IS PUNISHED

God's curse on Cain meant that the land would no longer produce crops for him. He was therefore condemned to spend his life wandering from place to place, looking for fertile land where he could grow his crops. Yet God showed mercy on Cain by putting a mark on him, which would protect him from being killed by anyone else.

Abel lies dead on the ground.

NOAH

Genesis, Chapters 6–7

Noah was a good man, who respected God and obeyed his commands. At the time, the rest of humankind had grown so wicked that God wished he had never made them. He decided to send a flood, to cover the whole earth and wipe out all life. But because Noah was good, God chose to spare him and his family. He told Noah to build a great wooden ark, which would provide shelter from the flood for him and his family, as well as for two of every type of living creature. The ark would protect them from the flood.

Ham

The animals make their way to the ark.

According to the Bible, the ark is made of "gopher wood", most likely wood from the cypress tree.

TWO BY TWO
Noah was told to collect a male and female of every kind of living creature. In this way, the earth could be filled with life again after the flood.

Noah's three sons help him build the ark.

CHAPTER 6 VERSE 22
"Noah did everything just as God commanded him."
Noah's unquestioning obedience to God shows why he is chosen to survive the flood.

Shem

Japheth

Noah builds the ark, following God's detailed instructions.

Noah

THE FLOOD AND THE RAINBOW
Genesis, Chapters 7–9

It rained for forty days and forty nights, and the waters rose up to cover the whole earth. Then at last, God stopped the rain from falling, and sent a wind to push the waters back. The ark came to rest on the mountains of Ararat. But there was still water as far as the eye could see, so Noah and his family had to stay inside the ark. Noah only learned that there was dry land when he sent out a dove, which flew back to the ark with an olive leaf in its beak. This meant there was now enough dry land for Noah, his family, and all the creatures to finally come out of the ark.

The dove flies back to Noah with an olive leaf.

THE WATERS RISE
The flood lasted for a hundred and fifty days. The water had risen so high that it covered even the tallest mountains. Every living thing on land drowned. Only Noah, his family, and the animals in the ark were safe.

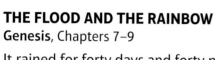

The Old Testament

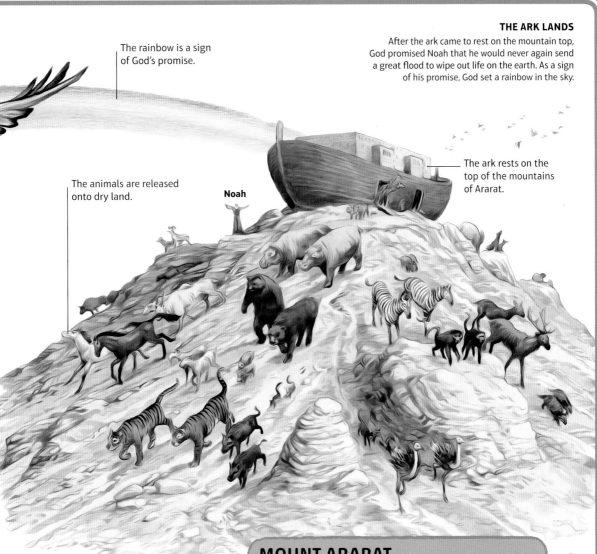

The rainbow is a sign of God's promise.

THE ARK LANDS

After the ark came to rest on the mountain top, God promised Noah that he would never again send a great flood to wipe out life on the earth. As a sign of his promise, God set a rainbow in the sky.

The ark rests on the top of the mountains of Ararat.

The animals are released onto dry land.

Noah

Today, the dove with an olive branch is seen as a **symbol of peace**.

MOUNT ARARAT

In the Bible, the "mountains of Ararat" refers to a region rather than a particular peak. However, Mount Ararat in Turkey (below) has long been identified as the place where the ark came to rest.

THE TOWER OF BABEL
Genesis, Chapter 11

After the great flood, the earth gradually filled with people again. They all spoke the same language and could easily understand each other. Moving east, they settled in a wide plain in Shinar. Here they decided to build a city, with a tower so tall that it would reach heaven. They set about building the tower, and it rose to the sky. But God was not pleased with the people's pride and desire for glory. He confused their speech, making each person speak a different language. Suddenly the air was filled with a babble of languages and nobody could understand each other.

The great tower reaches to the sky.

Nimrod, king of Shinar, oversees the building of the tower.

BABEL

Unable to communicate with each other, the people stopped building the city and named it Babel – which sounds like the Hebrew word for "confusion". Babel is probably based on the great city of Babylon, which was famous for its tall temple, called a ziggurat.

MUD BRICKS

The builders of the Tower of Babel used sun-dried mud bricks, which are still used as a building material in many parts of the Middle East. Unlike Israel, which is a rocky land, Babylonia had no suitable stone for building.

"Shinar" is the Hebrew name for "Babylonia", an ancient region which is now in Iraq.

The people can no longer understand each other.

THE PEOPLE SCATTER

No longer able to work together on the tower, many people scattered over the face of the earth, speaking many different languages. According to the Bible, this is why different languages are spoken in different parts of the world.

ABRAHAM
Genesis, Chapters 11-12

There was a man called Abram (Abraham) who lived in the land of Harran in Mesopotamia, where he owned flocks of sheep, goats, and cattle. One day God spoke to Abram and told him to leave his homeland, and travel south-west to Canaan. God said that Abram would be the forefather of a great nation. Even though Abram was 75 years old, and had no children, he believed in God's promise. He told his family and servants to pack up their belongings, and they all set off towards Canaan. Abram is better known as Abraham, the name he was given by God later in his life.

The name "Abraham" means **"father of many nations"**.

Abram

TO CANAAN
Abram did as God had told him, and began the long journey towards Canaan. Travelling with him were his wife Sarai (Sarah), his nephew Lot, their servants, and their flocks.

TREE OF MOREH

After arriving in Canaan, Abram reached a place called Moreh, where a great tree stood. Here God appeared to Abram, telling him that the whole land would one day be given to his children. In gratitude, Abram built an altar, a place where he could offer sacrifices to God.

CHAPTER 12 VERSE 6

"At that time the Canaanites were in the land."

Abram finds that the land promised to his children is already occupied. Unable to stay, he continues his journey to Negev, south of Canaan.

Abram kneels in prayer before the altar.

CHAPTER 12 VERSE 2

"I will make you into a great nation..."

God promises Abram that his children will become a great nation, later called the Israelites, and that he will give them the land of Canaan.

THE ANCIENT CITY OF UR

According to the Bible, Abram was born in the city of Ur in Mesopotamia (modern-day Iraq). At its centre stood a vast temple called a ziggurat, which has been partly restored.

The Old Testament

LOT
Genesis, Chapters 18-19

God sent two angels, who looked like men, to the city of Sodom. The people of Sodom, and those of its neighbouring city Gomorrah, were known for their wickedness. God told Abram (Abraham) that he planned to destroy both cities. But Abram, whose nephew Lot lived in Sodom, pleaded with God to spare the place. He reminded God that good people also lived there. God agreed that, if his angels could find ten good people in Sodom, he would spare the city for their sake. At nightfall, the angels reached the city, where Lot welcomed them.

There is a **real pillar of salt** called **"Lot's wife"** on Mount Sodom, in Israel.

THE ANGRY CROWD

That evening, all the men of Sodom came to Lot's house, and demanded that he hand over his guests to them. Lot knew they meant to harm the angels, and refused, so they threatened to break down his door. The angels then struck the men outside blind.

LOT AND THE ANGELS

Outside the gates of Sodom, the angels were met by Lot, who invited them to stay with him. They said they wished to stay in the city square, but Lot insisted that they go home with him as his guests.

Sodom is destroyed by fire and brimstone (burning sulfur).

Lot's wife is turned into a pillar of salt.

Lot flees with his wife and daughters.

SODOM IS DESTROYED

Lot and his family fled for their lives, while God rained down fire on Sodom and Gomorrah. Lot's wife forgot the angels' warning, and turned round to look at the city. For this, she was turned into a pillar of salt.

THE ANGELS' WARNING

The angels told Lot that Sodom and Gomorrah would both be destroyed by God the very next day. They told Lot and his family to flee, and warned them not to look back at Sodom.

The angel tells Lot to leave the city and head to the mountains.

CHAPTER 19 VERSE 8

"... they have come under the protection of my roof."

Lot risks his own life to protect his guests, even though they are strangers, and he does not realize that they are angels. His actions show that he is a good man, and so he is saved by God.

❖

CHAPTER 19 VERSE 26

"But Lot's wife looked back, and she became a pillar of salt."

Lot's wife could not resist having one last look at the city. She is punished for disobeying the angels.

The Old Testament

SARAH

Genesis, Chapters 17-18

When Abram was 99 years old, God came to him and renewed his promise that Abram would be the father of many nations. He gave Abram and his wife, Sarai, new names – Abraham and Sarah. God said that Sarah would give birth to a son, and Abraham laughed at the idea, as his wife was 90 years old. Later, Abraham was sitting by his tent when three strangers approached. One of them was God, who told Abraham that a year later Sarah would indeed give birth to a son. Just as God had promised, Sarah later gave birth to a boy, who was named Isaac.

CHAPTER 17 VERSE 4

"... this is my covenant with you..."

God makes a new covenant, a formal agreement, with Abraham. He promises to watch over his children, and give them the land of Canaan.

CHAPTER 17 VERSE 15

"... her name will be Sarah."

Sarah, along with Abraham, is given a new name by God to highlight her status as an ancestor of God's chosen people, the Israelites. Both Sarai and Sarah mean "princess" in Hebrew.

SARAH LAUGHS

Coming out of their tent, Sarah overheard the stranger say that she would give birth to a son. Sarah laughed at the idea. Later, when her son was born, her disbelief turned to joy. Her son's name, Isaac, is a play on a Hebrew word meaning "to laugh".

God has appeared in human form.

Abraham shows his visitors hospitality.

Sarah laughs when she overhears the conversation.

Sarah

ISHMAEL
Genesis, Chapter 21

WATER IN THE DESERT

When the water they carried ran out, Hagar and Ishmael sat under a bush and wept. God heard them weeping, and showed Hagar where to find a well. She filled the waterskin, and brought it to Ishmael to drink.

Ishmael was Abraham's first son, born to Hagar, Sarah's Egyptian slave girl. After Sarah gave birth to Isaac, she grew to dislike Ishmael. One day, Sarah found Ishmael making fun of Isaac. In a fury, she told Abraham to get rid of Ishmael and his mother. Abraham, who loved his first son, did not want to send him away. But God told Abraham to listen to Sarah, promising that he would protect Hagar and Ishmael. Abraham gave the pair some food and a skin full of water, and they went out into the desert.

Ishmael had **twelve sons, each** of whom **founded their own tribe**.

CHAPTER 21 VERSE 13

"I will make the son of the slave into a nation also..."

God promises Abraham that Ishmael will be the father of a nation in his own right. His children were the Ishmaelites, the desert people who lived east and south of Canaan. Many Arabs today trace their descent back to Ishmael.

ABRAHAM'S TEST
Genesis, Chapters 21–22

Abraham is delighted with baby Isaac.

Abraham and Sarah were full of joy at the birth of their son, Isaac. Some time later, God spoke to Abraham again, to test his faith. He told Abraham to take Isaac to the region of Moriah. There God would show him a mountain on which Abraham should build an altar and sacrifice his son as a burnt offering. With a heavy heart, Abraham took Isaac, two servants, and a donkey, and set off to Moriah. When Abraham told his son that they were going to make an offering to God, Isaac asked, "Where is the lamb that we are going to sacrifice?" Abraham told him that God would provide one.

MOUNTAINS OF MORIAH
When they reached Moriah, Abraham told his servants to stay behind with the donkey, while he and Isaac went up the mountain to worship.

Isaac carries a bundle of wood to build a fire on the altar.

Abraham carries the fire for the offering.

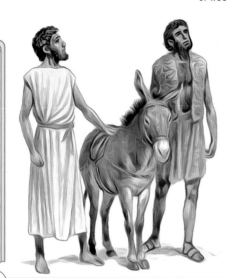

THE ALTAR

Abraham built an altar and placed wood on it. He bound Isaac and laid him on top. When Abraham raised a knife to strike his son, an angel appeared and told him not to hurt Isaac. The angel explained that God had tested Abraham's faith.

Isaac lies patiently on the altar.

Abraham

Angel

RAM IN THE THICKET

Abraham sees a ram caught in a thicket and sacrifices it instead of Isaac.

CHAPTER 22 VERSE 12

"Now I know that you fear God..."

The angel tells Abraham that he has passed God's test. His willingness to sacrifice Isaac shows that he places God above everything else.

REBEKAH
Genesis, Chapter 24

Rebekah comes to collect water.

The camels are carrying gifts from Abraham for his future daughter-in-law.

The servant waits by the well.

Rebekah

As a very old man, Abraham wanted to find a wife for his beloved son Isaac. He sent his most trusted servant back to Mesopotamia, his original homeland, to find a woman from his own people. When the servant arrived, he waited by a well, and prayed to God to help him find a bride for Isaac. Soon a beautiful young woman, called Rebekah, arrived. She was the granddaughter of Abraham's brother and the answer to the servant's prayer.

AT THE WELL

Waiting at the well, the servant prayed that the woman who was right for Isaac would offer him a drink of water. When Rebekah arrived, she offered water to the servant and his camels. It appeared that God had chosen Rebekah for Isaac.

CHAPTER 24 VERSE 58
"'I will go,' she said."
After the servant gives Rebekah gifts from Abraham and tells her of his prayer, she agrees it is God's will that she marries Isaac. She goes to Canaan to be his wife.

ISAAC
Genesis, Chapter 25

When Abraham died, at the age of 175, Isaac became the head of the family. He loved his wife Rebekah dearly, and she was a comfort to him after his parents died. Yet, for twenty years after they married, Isaac and Rebekah were childless. They prayed to God for help, and at last Rebekah became pregnant, with twins. She grew alarmed when she felt the babies jostling inside her. God told her that this was because their boys would grow up to found two rival nations, and that one nation would be stronger than the other.

CHAPTER 25 VERSE 23
"Two nations are in your womb..."
The two nations Isaac's sons will establish will be Israel, founded by Jacob, and Edom, founded by Esau. Israel will be stronger than Edom.

CHAPTER 25 VERSE 26
"... his brother came out, with his hand grasping Esau's heel..."
Grasping someone by the heel is a way of tripping them. Jacob will use cunning to become more powerful than Esau.

Isaac

Rebekah

Jacob has dark hair, unlike his elder brother.

TWINS
Isaac and Rebekah's twin boys looked nothing like each other. The firstborn, who was red and covered with hair, was named Esau, meaning "hairy". He was Isaac's favourite. The second boy was born holding onto his brother's heel, so they called him Jacob, meaning "heel-catcher". He was Rebekah's favourite.

JACOB

Genesis, Chapters 25–27

Esau

Jacob

Though twins, Jacob and Esau were very different. While Jacob helped their mother Rebekah with her work, and was her favourite, Esau hunted animals with a bow and arrow, and was Isaac's favourite. Esau was the firstborn, which meant he would become head of the family when Isaac died. As part of his birthright, Esau would receive God's promise to Abraham – that his descendants would be given the Promised Land. But Esau did not value his birthright. One day, when he was hungry, he sold his birthright to Jacob for a bowl of lentil stew.

SELLING THE BIRTHRIGHT
Esau came home one day after hunting, hungry for food. He asked for the lentil stew Jacob was stirring. When Jacob demanded Esau's birthright in return, Esau foolishly agreed.

Isaac asks Esau to prepare a special meal for him.

Rebekah overhears the conversation, and decides to help Jacob receive Isaac's blessing.

DESERT LIFE

Isaac's family lived in tents, in Beersheba, which is in the desert country to the south of Canaan. In parts of the Middle East, people still live in tents, travelling from one grazing place or water hole to another with their sheep and goats.

By **selling his birthright**, Esau showed he **did not deserve it**.

JACOB IS BLESSED

When Isaac grew old, he asked Esau to make him his favourite meal, so he could give Esau his blessings. Rebekah, however, favoured Jacob. While Esau was out hunting, Rebekah told Jacob to disguise himself as his brother. Wearing Esau's clothes and hairy goatskin on his hands, Jacob fooled Issac, who was now blind, into thinking he was Esau, and Isaac blessed Jacob instead.

Esau goes to hunt for food for Isaac.

Jacob, disguised as Esau, is blessed.

Isaac feels Jacob's hands, covered with goatskin, and mistakes him for Esau.

JACOB'S FLIGHT
Genesis, Chapters 28–29

When Esau found out that Jacob had received Isaac's blessing, he was so angry that he planned to kill his brother. On learning of this, Rebekah told Jacob to run away to her brother Laban, who lived in Harran in Mesopotamia. Jacob set off on his journey, but stopped to sleep for the night when the sun had set. He placed a smooth stone under his head as a pillow, and soon fell asleep. As he slept, Jacob dreamed of a great stairway rising into the sky, with angels walking up and down it. At the very top of those stairs, he saw God.

Jacob later **returned** and built an **altar in Bethel**.

Jacob sleeps

GOD'S PROMISE
In his dream, Jacob saw God at the top of the stairway. God promised Jacob that he would one day give him the land on which he was lying. God said, "I will bring you back to this land."

JACOB'S STAIRWAY

In his dream, Jacob sees a stairway rising into the sky. This description of the stairway may be based on a Mesopotamian ziggurat, a giant stepped pyramid, which has a flight of stairs leading to a shrine at the top. Shown here is the ziggurat at Ur, in Iraq.

Angels walk up and down the stairway.

Jacob's uncle Laban rushes out to greet him.

Rachel

THE HOUSE OF GOD

On waking from his dream, Jacob took the stone he had slept on and set it up as a pillar. He poured oil on it, and vowed that if God allowed him to return, he would build an altar there. He called the place Bethel, meaning "the house of God".

Jacob pours oil on the stone as an offering to God.

JACOB AND RACHEL

When Jacob reached Harran, he met Laban's daughter, Rachel, who had brought sheep to the well to be watered. Jacob fell in love with her at first sight, and he kissed her.

Jacob sets the stone up to mark the holy site.

LEAH AND RACHEL
Genesis, Chapters 29-30

Laban

Leah

Rachel

THE WRONG BRIDE
Jacob fell in love with Rachel at first sight, but waited seven years to marry her. However, when the time came for their wedding, Laban presented Leah, who was wearing a veil, as Jacob's bride instead of Rachel. He tricked Jacob because at the time it was not the custom for a younger daughter to be married before an older one. As Leah's face was covered, Jacob did not know that he had been cheated.

Jacob asks for Rachel's hand in marriage.

Leah and Rachel were the daughters of Laban, Jacob's uncle. After he fled from his brother Esau, Jacob came to stay with them in Harran. Jacob fell in love with the younger daughter, Rachel, who was more beautiful than Leah. Laban was pleased to have Jacob help him with his work, and offered to pay him wages. Jacob said he would work without wages for seven years, if he could marry Rachel. Laban agreed, and after the seven years, he held a great feast for the wedding. However, Laban tricked Jacob into marrying Leah instead of Rachel.

CHAPTER 29 VERSE 25
"Why have you deceived me?"
Jacob is angry with Laban for tricking him into marrying Leah. Yet Jacob tricked his own brother, Esau, out of his birthright. The trickster is tricked.

⟡

CHAPTER 30 VERSE 1
"... she became jealous of her sister."
Rachel is jealous of Leah's ability to bear children. Leah is also jealous of her sister, because she knows that Jacob loves Rachel more than her.

TWO WIVES

During their first night together, it was too dark for Jacob to see his bride. So it was only the next morning that he realized he had married Leah, not Rachel. When confronted about this, Laban promised Jacob that he could also marry Rachel, if he would work for another seven years. Jacob agreed, and a week after marrying Leah, he married Rachel.

Jacob is shocked to see Leah beside him.

Leah

Jacob's twelve sons founded the **Twelve Tribes of Israel**.

Leah gives Jacob six sons and a daughter.

Jacob

Rachel holds Joseph, the first of her two sons.

JACOB'S CHILDREN

Jacob had twelve sons and a daughter by his wives and their maidservants, Zilpah and Bilhah. Leah gave Jacob seven children, but he still loved Rachel more, though it was years before she gave birth to her first baby, Joseph.

Bilhah has two sons.

Zilpah has two sons.

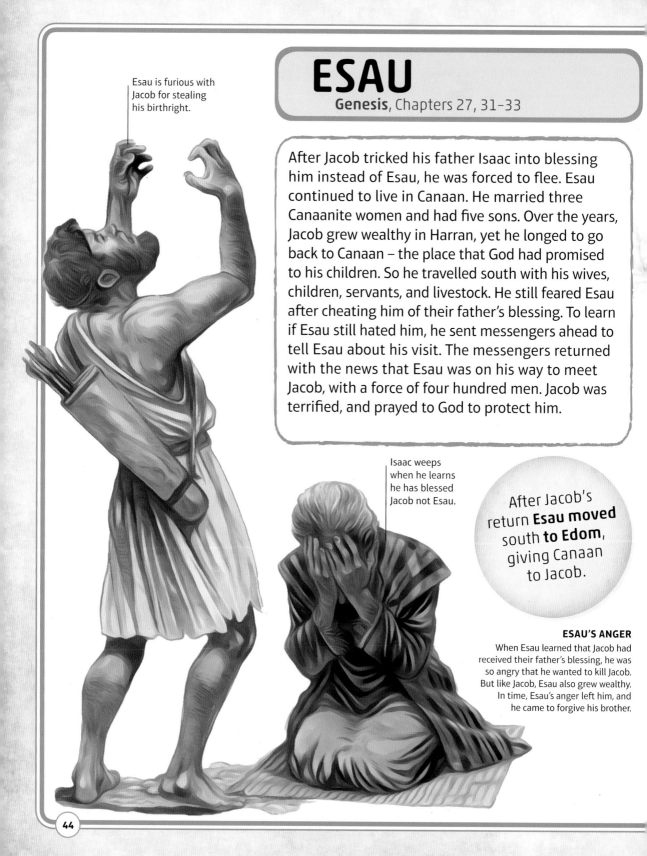

Esau is furious with Jacob for stealing his birthright.

ESAU
Genesis, Chapters 27, 31–33

After Jacob tricked his father Isaac into blessing him instead of Esau, he was forced to flee. Esau continued to live in Canaan. He married three Canaanite women and had five sons. Over the years, Jacob grew wealthy in Harran, yet he longed to go back to Canaan – the place that God had promised to his children. So he travelled south with his wives, children, servants, and livestock. He still feared Esau after cheating him of their father's blessing. To learn if Esau still hated him, he sent messengers ahead to tell Esau about his visit. The messengers returned with the news that Esau was on his way to meet Jacob, with a force of four hundred men. Jacob was terrified, and prayed to God to protect him.

Isaac weeps when he learns he has blessed Jacob not Esau.

After Jacob's return **Esau moved** south **to Edom**, giving Canaan to Jacob.

ESAU'S ANGER
When Esau learned that Jacob had received their father's blessing, he was so angry that he wanted to kill Jacob. But like Jacob, Esau also grew wealthy. In time, Esau's anger left him, and he came to forgive his brother.

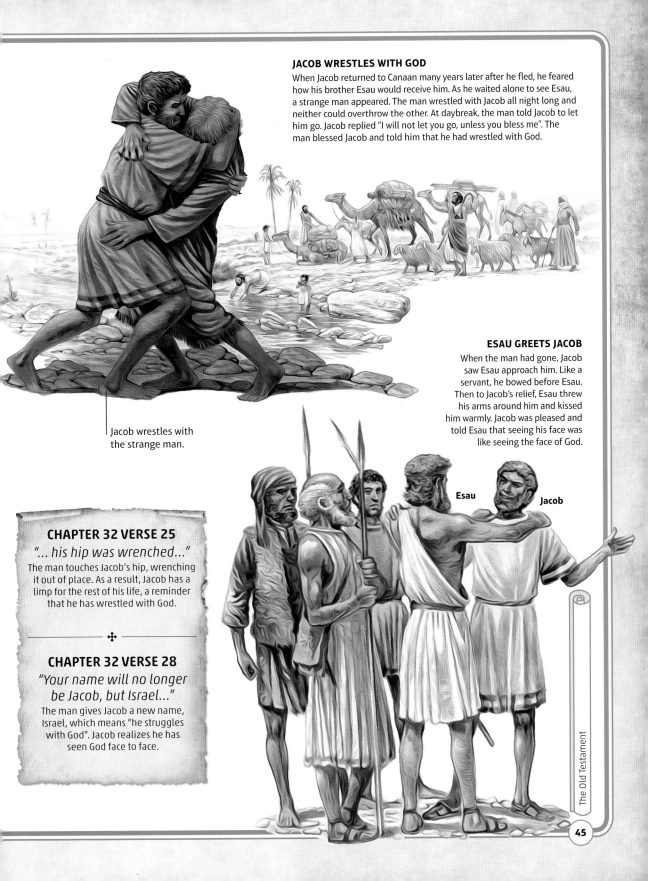

JACOB WRESTLES WITH GOD

When Jacob returned to Canaan many years later after he fled, he feared how his brother Esau would receive him. As he waited alone to see Esau, a strange man appeared. The man wrestled with Jacob all night long and neither could overthrow the other. At daybreak, the man told Jacob to let him go. Jacob replied "I will not let you go, unless you bless me". The man blessed Jacob and told him that he had wrestled with God.

Jacob wrestles with the strange man.

ESAU GREETS JACOB

When the man had gone, Jacob saw Esau approach him. Like a servant, he bowed before Esau. Then to Jacob's relief, Esau threw his arms around him and kissed him warmly. Jacob was pleased and told Esau that seeing his face was like seeing the face of God.

Esau

Jacob

CHAPTER 32 VERSE 25

"... his hip was wrenched..."

The man touches Jacob's hip, wrenching it out of place. As a result, Jacob has a limp for the rest of his life, a reminder that he has wrestled with God.

CHAPTER 32 VERSE 28

"Your name will no longer be Jacob, but Israel..."

The man gives Jacob a new name, Israel, which means "he struggles with God". Jacob realizes he has seen God face to face.

JOSEPH

Genesis, Chapters 37, 39

The son of Jacob and Rachel, Joseph lived in Canaan with his parents and brothers. He was the favourite son of Jacob, who showed his love for Joseph by giving him a beautiful coat. This made Joseph's brothers jealous. Then Joseph told his brothers about two of his dreams, in which his brothers had bowed down before him. Thinking that this meant Joseph planned to rule over them, they disliked him even more. To get rid of Joseph, his brothers threw him into a pit, and then sold him as a slave to some travelling merchants.

Colourful robes were highly valued in Canaan.

THE COLOURFUL COAT

Joseph's coat had long sleeves and was richly decorated, with cloth woven from many colours. Joseph wore it all the time, which was a constant reminder to his brothers that he was their father's favourite son. The first thing they did when they seized Joseph was to strip him of his coat.

Jacob   **Joseph**

Reuben anxiously watches his brothers throw Joseph into the pit.

Joseph had **eleven brothers** and **one sister**.

THROWN INTO A PIT

At first, Joseph's brothers planned to kill him, and hide his body in a pit. But Reuben, who was the kindest brother, convinced the others not to kill Joseph but to throw him into the pit alive. The brothers told their father Jacob that Joseph had been killed by a wild animal. As proof, they showed their father Joseph's coat, which they had smeared with goat's blood.

SOLD AS A SLAVE

Later that day, the brothers saw a caravan of Ishmaelite merchants passing by, with camels loaded with goods. Joseph's brothers pulled him out of the pit, and sold him to the Ishmaelites for silver. They thought that they had seen the last of Joseph. The merchants travelled on to Egypt, where they sold Joseph in a market as a slave.

The Ishmaelites were desert Arabs, thought to be the descendants of Abraham's son, Ishmael.

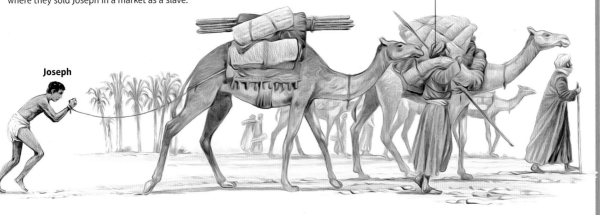

Joseph

The brothers take Joseph's coat.

The brothers throw Joseph into the pit without food or water.

CHAPTER 37 VERSE 20

"... we'll see what comes of his dreams."

Joseph dreams that his brothers' sheaves of corn and the sun, moon, and stars bow down to him. To his brothers, this appears to mean that Joseph plans to rule over them.

✥

CHAPTER 39 VERSE 2

"The Lord was with Joseph..."

In Egypt, God protects Joseph, just as he watched over Abraham, Isaac, and Jacob. Thanks to God's protection, Joseph rises to a position of importance. His dream that his brothers bow down to him will come true.

Joseph explains their dreams.

Cupbearer

Baker

THE SERVANTS' DREAMS

The imprisoned servants told Joseph their dreams. The cupbearer dreamed he was squeezing grapes into Pharaoh's cup. Joseph told him that this meant he would get his job back. The baker dreamed that birds were pecking at loaves of bread on his head. Joseph said this meant he would be hanged, and birds would peck at his body.

JOSEPH IN EGYPT
Genesis, Chapters 39–41

In Egypt, Joseph was sold as a slave to Potiphar, a royal official. Potiphar's wife asked Joseph to be her lover, but he refused. She was so angry with Joseph that she falsely accused him of a crime, and had him thrown into prison. The prison warden liked Joseph, and put him in charge of the other prisoners. While Joseph was in there, Pharaoh also imprisoned two of his servants – his cupbearer and his baker. One morning they awoke after having strange dreams. Joseph told them that their dreams meant that the cupbearer would be freed, but the baker would be hanged.

In Egypt, a king was called "pharaoh", meaning "great house".

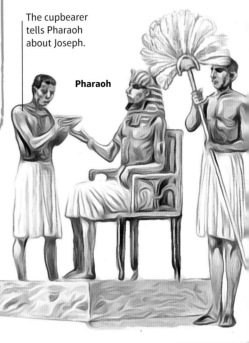

The cupbearer tells Pharaoh about Joseph.

Pharaoh

PHARAOH'S DREAM

As Joseph foretold, the baker was hanged and the cupbearer freed to serve Pharaoh again. Two years later, the cupbearer heard Pharaoh speak of a worrying dream he had had. The cupbearer then remembered Joseph, and told Pharaoh, who sent for Joseph to explain what his dream meant.

Joseph

JOSEPH EXPLAINS THE DREAM

In his dream, Pharaoh saw seven fat cows coming out of the River Nile. They were followed by seven thin cows, which ate the fat cows. Joseph explained that there would be seven years of plenty, followed by seven years of famine. Joseph then advised Pharaoh to store up grain to prepare for the famine. Pharaoh was so impressed that he made Joseph his chief minister.

EGYPTIAN GRANARY

This is a model of an Egyptian granary, used to store grain. There was usually a good harvest in Egypt, thanks to the yearly flooding of the River Nile. But if the river water was too low and did not flood, famine would follow.

MOSES

Exodus, Chapters 1–4

A NURSE FOR MOSES

While Moses was hidden in the reeds, he was watched over by his sister Miriam. When she saw that Pharaoh's daughter had found the baby, Miriam offered to bring a nurse. She came back with her mother, and Pharaoh's daughter asked the woman to nurse the infant. So Moses was raised by his real mother until he was older, when he was adopted by Pharaoh's daughter as her son.

Pharaoh's daughter finds the baby.

Moses' mother offers to nurse the baby.

Miriam

"Moses" is an **Egyptian name** meaning "born of".

As the years passed, the Israelites spread in great numbers throughout Egypt. The new Pharaoh (king) feared having so many foreign people in his land. So he forced the Israelites to work as his slaves. Then he gave orders for every newborn Israelite boy to be thrown into the River Nile. An Israelite woman from the tribe of Levi hid her baby boy in the bulrushes, or reeds, along the river. Here the boy was found by Pharaoh's daughter, who took him home to raise him. She called the boy Moses. Although he had an Egyptian upbringing, Moses never forgot that he was an Israelite.

MOUNT HOREB

The location of the biblical Mount Horeb, also known as Mount Sinai, is not known. There is an old tradition that it is the mountain shown here, Jebel Musa. Jebel Musa is in Egypt and is 2,286-m- (7,500-ft-) high. Its name means "mountain of Moses" in Arabic.

»

CHAPTER 3 VERSE 14
"I am who I am."
God tells Moses that his name is "Yahweh", a name based on the phrase "I am who I am." Jews consider this to be God's holiest name, and do not speak it aloud.

CHAPTER 4 VERSE 13
"Please send someone else."
Moses feels that the task set by God, to free the Israelites, is too difficult. God says he will watch over Moses, and suggests that if Moses feels he cannot, he should ask his brother Aaron to speak for him.

GOD SPEAKS TO MOSES

Later, as an adult, Moses killed an Egyptian he saw hitting an Israelite. He then fled Egypt and went to live in Midian. One day, when Moses was on Mount Horeb, he saw a bush on fire. From the burning bush, God spoke to Moses, asking him to go back to Egypt to free the Israelites from slavery.

God speaks to Moses from a burning bush.

Moses asks God what name should he give for him to the Israelites.

THE PLAGUES AND THE EXODUS
Exodus, Chapters 5–14

Moses returned to Egypt and asked Pharaoh to let the Israelites go, but he refused. So God struck Egypt with ten terrible plagues. First the waters of the River Nile turned into blood. The other plagues included plagues of frogs, locusts, and flies. In the ninth plague, total darkness covered the country for three days. For the tenth plague, God struck every firstborn Egyptian male dead. At this, Pharaoh finally agreed to let the Israelites go.

RIVER OF BLOOD
For the first plague, God asked Moses to tell his brother Aaron to strike the waters of the River Nile with his staff. When Aaron did this, the water turned into stinking blood. All the fish died, and the Egyptians could not drink the water. Despite this, Pharaoh refused to free the Israelites.

The water becomes stinking blood.

Swarms of flies persecute the Egyptians.

SWARMS OF FLIES
In the fourth plague, swarms of flies filled every Egyptian house. To bring it to an end, Pharaoh agreed to Moses' demands. However, once all the flies had died, Pharaoh changed his mind.

PLAGUE OF LOCUSTS
For the eighth plague, locusts covered the ground so thickly that it looked black. The locusts ate every plant in the country. Only Goshen, the part of Egypt where the Israelites lived, was spared.

EXODUS FROM EGYPT

When Pharaoh finally let the Israelites go, they left Egypt in such a hurry that they had no time for their bread to rise. They were led by God, who moved before them in a pillar of cloud. But, Pharaoh wished he had not let the Israelites go and chased after them with his army.

God leads Moses and the Israelites.

"Exodus" is a **Greek word** meaning **"going out"**.

The women carry unrisen dough.

PARTING THE SEA

Pharaoh's army caught up with the Israelites on the shores of the Red Sea. God told Moses to raise his hand over the sea. When Moses did this, the waters parted, leaving a path of dry ground for the Israelites to cross. The Egyptian army tried to follow, but the waters came crashing down, drowning them.

All the Egyptians are drowned at sea.

GATHERING MANNA
God told Moses that he would rain down bread from heaven. This bread took the form of white flakes, which tasted like wafers made of honey. The Israelites, who had never seen such food before, called it manna.

The Israelites collect the white flakes in baskets.

FOOD IN THE DESERT
Exodus, Chapters 16–23

After crossing the Red Sea, the Israelites found themselves in a hot, dry desert, which they would have to cross before they could reach the Promised Land of Canaan. They complained that there was nothing to eat or drink there, and they wished they had never left Egypt. But God told Moses that he would look after the Israelites. First he sent a flock of quails, which dropped to the ground around them. Then he rained down a type of bread, which the people called manna. The Israelites lived on manna for all of the forty years it took them to reach the Promised Land.

Moses strikes the rock with his staff.

WATER FROM A ROCK
The Israelites reached Horeb, where God had spoken to Moses years before from the burning bush. Now God told Moses to strike a rock with his staff. When he did this, a stream of clear water flowed out, and there was enough for everyone to drink.

"Manna" is a Hebrew word meaning **"what is it?"**

THE TEN COMMANDMENTS
Exodus, Chapter 20

God appeared as a great fire burning on Mount Sinai, and told Moses to go up and meet him at the top. When Moses went up, God gave him a set of laws, called the Ten Commandments. The most important commandment was to worship no other gods. Alongside the commandments, God gave Moses many other rules, which covered religious worship and daily life. God said that, if the Israelites kept his laws, he would protect them.

God appears on Mount Sinai as a fire and speaks to Moses. ———————

ON THE MOUNTAIN
After giving the laws to Moses, God gave him two stone tablets with the Ten Commandments written on them. He also told Moses to build a gold-plated wooden box, called the Ark of the Covenant, to hold the tablets.

THE TEN COMMANDMENTS

1 You shall have no other gods before me.

2 You shall not make for yourself an idol.

3 You shall not misuse the name of the Lord your God.

4 Remember the Sabbath day by keeping it holy.

5 Honour your father and your mother.

6 You shall not murder.

7 You shall not commit adultery.

8 You shall not steal.

9 You shall not give false testimony against your neighbour.

10 You shall not covet... anything that belongs to your neighbour.

The Old Testament

AARON

Exodus, Chapters 4, 24, 32

Aaron

Aaron was Moses' older brother, and a prophet. He helped Moses guide the Israelites out of Egypt. When the Israelites reached Mount Sinai, God told Moses to go up the mountain to meet him. Moses left Aaron in charge of the people and went up the mountain. Moses was away for such a long time that the Israelites thought he was never coming back. So they went to Aaron, and asked him to make them a god to worship. Aaron collected all their gold jewellery, and melted the gold to make a statue of the calf.

MOSES AND AARON

Moses hated making speeches, but Aaron, who was three years older, was a good speaker. So Moses used his brother as his spokesman. Aaron was also the first High Priest of Israel.

The Israelites offer Aaron their gold jewellery.

ON MOUNT SINAI

Moses spent forty days and forty nights on Mount Sinai, where God gave him a series of laws. The most important of these were the Ten Commandments, written on two stone tablets. The second commandment banned worshipping idols, which are statues or images of a god.

CHAPTER 32 VERSE 35

"And the Lord struck the people with a plague..."

God punishes the Israelites with a plague for worshipping the calf. But he later tells Moses to continue to lead them to the Promised Land.

Moses angrily smashes the stone tablets.

The Israelites worship the golden calf.

GATHERING GOLD

Aaron collected the gold jewellery from the Israelites and made the statue of a calf. He built an altar in front of it and the Israelites made sacrifices and presented offerings to their golden calf idol.

THE ANGER OF MOSES

When Moses finally returned from the mountain with the stone tablets, he found the Israelites dancing in front of the golden calf. He was so angry that he threw the tablets to the ground, smashing them. Aaron had let the Israelites run out of control, and Moses was furious with him. Later, Moses had to go back up Mount Sinai with new tablets to receive the Ten Commandments again.

APIS, THE BULL GOD

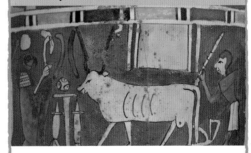

Many ancient peoples worshipped bulls, who were prized because of their great strength. The Egyptians honoured the bull god Apis, shown in this painting, by worshipping a living bull as the god. The god's temple in Egypt was filled with statues of bulls.

The Old Testament

MIRIAM
Numbers, Chapter 12

Miriam was Moses' older sister, who had protected him in Egypt when he was a baby. While the Israelites were travelling in the wilderness, Miriam grew jealous of Moses. With her brother Aaron, she questioned Moses' right to lead the Israelites, saying that they were prophets too, for God also spoke to them. God was angered at their words, and he appeared to them as a pillar of cloud. He said that he only spoke directly to Moses, and that they were wrong to challenge their brother.

CHAPTER 12 VERSE 3

"... Moses was a very humble man, more humble than anyone else..."

Moses' humbleness contrasts with Miriam and Aaron. Unlike Moses, they care more about their own importance than obeying God's will.

✢

CHAPTER 12 VERSE 6

"When there is a prophet among you, I, the lord... speak to them in dreams."

God says that the usual way he speaks to prophets is by sending them dreams. But he speaks openly and directly only to Moses.

MIRIAM'S PUNISHMENT

When the cloud rose, Miriam had been struck with a skin disease. God had punished her for challenging Moses. But Moses forgave her and cried out for God's help. Miriam was cured.

God appears as a pillar of cloud.

Aaron

Miriam

Moses

BALAAM

Numbers, Chapters 22–24

King Balak of Moab was terrified when he saw the Israelites approach his kingdom. He sent for Balaam, a seer (a type of prophet), and asked him to curse the Israelites. When Balaam set off on a donkey to do this, an angel appeared and blocked his path. The donkey saw the angel and turned off the path. When Balaam beat it for doing this, God gave the donkey speech and it asked Balaam why it deserved the beating. God then opened Balaam's eyes to the angel, who told him to do only what he instructed. God then made Balaam bless the Israelites instead of cursing them, making King Balak furious.

CHAPTER 22 VERSE 35

"Go with the men, but speak only what I tell you."

The angel allows Balaam to continue his journey to Moab, but tells him to say only what God puts into his mouth. Fearful of punishment, Balaam obeys.

CHAPTER 24 VERSE 17

"... a scepter will rise out of Israel."

A scepter is a decorated staff, held by a king as a sign of office. Balaam prophesies that the Israelites will one day have a great king, a reference to the future king David.

Unable to see the angel, Balaam beats his donkey.

SEER
Balaam was a seer, who was famous for his ability to curse and to bless. Though he was not an Israelite, he feared God, and could not resist his commands.

Balaam

Angel

The angel stands with a drawn sword, blocking Balaam's way.

JOSHUA

Joshua, Chapters 1–6

After Moses died, the Israelites were led by Joshua, a warrior and a prophet. God told Joshua to cross the River Jordan, and enter the Promised Land of Canaan. Joshua sent spies ahead, who returned and told him that the people of Canaan were terrified of the Israelites. The next day, encouraged by this good news, Joshua told the Israelites to cross the River Jordan, with priests carrying the Ark of the Covenant leading the way. God showed himself to be with the Israelites, for as soon as the priests stepped into the river, the water stopped flowing, and all the Israelites were able to cross on dry land.

CHAPTER 6 VERSE 21

"They devoted the city to the Lord…"

The Israelites offer the city of Jericho and everything in it to God, to thank him for the victory. They kill every living thing in the city as a sacrifice.

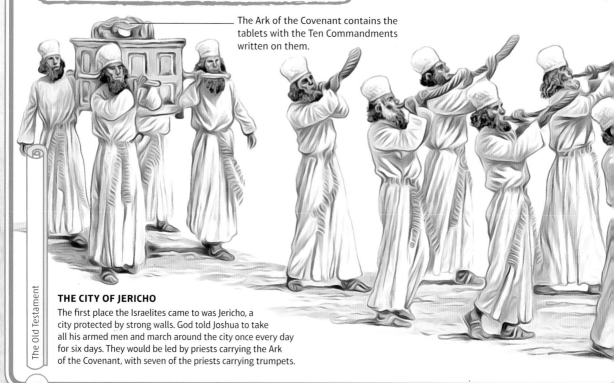

The Ark of the Covenant contains the tablets with the Ten Commandments written on them.

THE CITY OF JERICHO

The first place the Israelites came to was Jericho, a city protected by strong walls. God told Joshua to take all his armed men and march around the city once every day for six days. They would be led by priests carrying the Ark of the Covenant, with seven of the priests carrying trumpets.

At the sound of the trumpets, the walls collapse.

Joshua leads the Israelites into Jericho.

THE WALLS TUMBLE

God ordered that on the seventh day Joshua and his men march around the city seven times. The army marched around the city, then the priests blew a long blast on their trumpets, and all the people gave a loud shout. At this, the walls of Jericho came tumbling down. The Israelites rushed in and captured the city.

The Israelites kill every living thing in the city.

The **trumpets** used by the priests were **made of rams' horns**.

RUINS OF JERICHO

At Jericho, in Palestine, archaeologists have uncovered ruins dating back 10,000 years. Jericho was the world's first known walled town. Its walls fell many times, often due to earthquakes, and were rebuilt. Modern Jericho, alongside these ruins, is the oldest continuously inhabited city in the world.

The Old Testament

ACHAN PUNISHED

When Joshua asked people about the stolen treasure, Achan admitted to taking a robe and some silver and gold, which he had hidden in his tent. Joshua had the treasure brought out, and offered it to God. Achan and his family were then stoned to death, as punishment for stealing God's treasure.

Achan lies dead on the ground.

THE BATTLE OF AI
Joshua, Chapters 7–8

After capturing Jericho, Joshua led the Israelites to the city of Ai. He sent spies to Ai, who told Joshua that it was a small city, which could be captured with only a few thousand men. So Joshua sent a small force to attack Ai, but they were driven back. Joshua asked God why he had allowed them to be defeated. God said he was angry with the Israelites because one of them had taken treasure from Jericho for himself. On asking, a man called Achan confessed to Joshua that he had taken the treasure. This was given as an offering to God, ending his anger. God told Joshua to attack Ai again and that this time he would be successful.

Joshua lures the army of Ai away from the city.

God told Joshua to hold out his javelin as a signal for the attack.

BATTLE PLAN

After Achan's death, God was satisfied and told Joshua to attack Ai again by setting an ambush. So Joshua ordered thirty thousand of his best fighters to hide near the city during the night, and told them to wait for his signal before attacking the city. The next day, Joshua marched towards Ai with a smaller army.

Joshua

THE CITY OF AI

The city of Ai is popularly thought to be et-Tell, shown here. It matches the Bible's description of Ai, for it stands just 25 km (15 miles) northwest of Jericho, and was left in ruins in ancient times. However, archaeologists have learned that et-Tell was destroyed 1,000 years before Joshua's time.

THE FINAL BATTLE

Seeing only Joshua's small force, the army of Ai came running out to fight them. Joshua and his men fled, leading the enemy's forces away from their city, leaving the gates open. Joshua then signalled to the troops waiting in ambush to rush into the city and capture it. They burned Ai to the ground, leaving it a ruin.

The ambushers capture Ai and set it on fire.

The name **"Ai"** is Hebrew for **"ruin"**.

The fleeing Israelites turn on Ai's army when they see the city burning.

DEBORAH AND BARAK

Judges, Chapters 2–5

Statue of Baal

WORSHIPPING BAAL
Many Israelites began to worship Baal, the Canaanite rain god, preferring him to the God of Abraham and Moses. They thought Baal would help them by sending rain for their crops.

The Israelites settled in Canaan, and many of them began to worship the local gods. God punished them for this by allowing Canaanite raiders to attack the Israelites. Then, to save the Israelites, God gave them a series of leaders, called Judges, who tried to make the people keep God's laws. Deborah, a famous prophetess, was the only female Judge. Because God spoke through her, the Israelites asked her to sort out their quarrels. She held court beneath a tree, called the Palm of Deborah. To help the Israelites defeat the Canaanites, Deborah sent for Barak, a great Israelite commander.

Deborah tells Barak to lead the Israelites into battle.

Barak refuses to go without Deborah.

The Israelites attack the Canaanites.

DEBORAH CALLS FOR BARAK
Deborah sent for the Israelite commander, Barak, and asked him to lead a great army against the Canaanites and their commander, Sisera. Barak said he would go only if Deborah went with him. She agreed, but said that because of his request, God would hand Sisera over to a woman.

"Then the Lord raised up judges, who saved them…"

The word "Judge" is translated from the Hebrew word "Shophet", meaning "someone who decides". Shophets judged questions of law, but were also military leaders.

"… the Lord will deliver Sisera into the hands of a woman."

Deborah tells Barak that, because he wanted a woman to go into battle with him, he will also lose the honour of capturing the enemy commander to a woman.

DEBORAH'S SONG

The story of Deborah ends in her song of victory, shown here in this 19th-century engraving. It is one of the oldest poems in the Bible. The song gives a detailed description of the battle and praises Jael for killing Sisera. It finishes with a prayer to God, asking him to keep the Israelites strong.

The name **"Deborah"** means **"bee"** in Hebrew.

The Canaanites are killed by the Israelites.

Chariots get stuck in the mud.

Sisera runs away from the battle.

The battlefield is flooded by a storm sent by God.

SISERA IS KILLED

In a terrible battle, Barak's army killed all the Canaanites except Sisera, who ran away. He reached the tent of a woman called Jael, who offered him shelter. But Jael's tribe was friendly with the Israelites, and while Sisera slept, she killed him. In this way, the words of Deborah came true.

GIDEON

Judges, Chapters 6–7

Gideon

Gideon was a young Israelite who lived in Ophrah, a settlement in Canaan. At the time the Israelites had turned away from God and were worshipping other gods. To punish them, God allowed the Midianites, from Arabia, to invade the land. The Israelites suffered under the Midianites, crying out to God for help. God answered their prayers by sending an angel to Gideon. The angel told him God was with him, and that he was a mighty warrior who would save Israel. Under God's guidance and protection, Gideon destroyed the Israelite altars to false gods and led his people to victory.

THE ANGEL'S VISIT

The angel appeared to Gideon under the shade of an oak tree. Gideon brought him an offering of bread and meat, which the angel caused to burst into flames. Gideon knew this was a sign that he had been visited by an angel.

Asherah was the Canaanite **mother goddess**, associated with sacred trees.

Asherah poles were made of wood.

ASHERAH POLE

Following the angel's instructions, Gideon tore down the stone altar that his father had built to the god Baal. Taking an axe, he then chopped down the wooden pole dedicated to Asherah. Gideon replaced these with an altar to God.

Soldiers blow trumpets.

Soldiers carry torches.

NIGHT ATTACK

Gideon gathered an Israelite army. Although thousands of men wanted to join him, God told him to take only three hundred. With these men, Gideon attacked the Midianite camp at night. They made a loud noise by smashing empty jars and blowing on trumpets, and raised their torches. This made the Midianites panic and flee.

Gideon's men smash jars in which they were hiding their torches.

CHAPTER 7 VERSE 2

"You have too many men."

God tells Gideon to take only a small number of men. This is to teach the Israelites that their victory is from God.

❖

CHAPTER 7 VERSE 22

"When the three hundred trumpets sounded..."

The noise makes the Midianites think they are under attack from a big army. In the confusion, many draw their swords and accidentally kill each other.

CANAANITE ALTAR

These are the ruins of an altar at Megiddo, Israel, where the Canaanites worshipped gods, such as Baal and Asherah, in the open air. Canaanite altars, called "high places" in the Bible, were usually on hilltops. Many of them were destroyed by the Israelites.

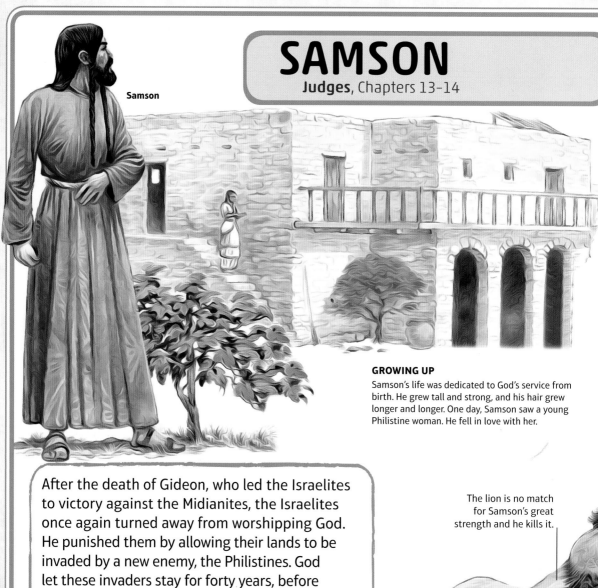

Samson

SAMSON
Judges, Chapters 13-14

GROWING UP
Samson's life was dedicated to God's service from birth. He grew tall and strong, and his hair grew longer and longer. One day, Samson saw a young Philistine woman. He fell in love with her.

After the death of Gideon, who led the Israelites to victory against the Midianites, the Israelites once again turned away from worshipping God. He punished them by allowing their lands to be invaded by a new enemy, the Philistines. God let these invaders stay for forty years, before sending the Israelites a new champion. An angel of God visited a man named Manoah, and told him that his wife would give birth to a son. The child would be a Nazirite – someone set apart as God's servant from birth – and his hair should never be cut. The child was named Samson.

The lion is no match for Samson's great strength and he kills it.

Nazirites were not allowed to cut their hair, drink alcohol, or touch a dead body.

CHAPTER 14 VERSE 14

"Out of the eater, something to eat; out of the strong, something sweet."

At his wedding, Samson asks the Philistine guests this riddle, the answer to which is "honey from a lion". Some of the Philistines threaten Samson's wife to get her to tell them the answer. When Samson finds out that she has told them, he angrily divorces her.

THE LION ATTACK

On his way to propose marriage to the Philistine woman, Samson was attacked by a lion. God gave Samson the strength to kill the lion with his bare hands. Samson then visited the woman, who agreed to be his wife.

EATING THE HONEY

Returning to marry the Philistine woman some days later, Samson found that bees had nested in the lion's carcass, and had made honey. He knelt down to eat some of the honey, even though this meant touching a dead body, a forbidden act for a Nazirite. Later, at his wedding feast, Samson challenged the Philistines to answer a riddle. They were baffled and threatened Samson's new wife so that she would tell them the answer.

Samson eats the honey.

DELILAH

Judges, Chapter 16

The Israelites' mighty champion Samson fell in love with a beautiful woman called Delilah. Samson was known for his strength, which he had used to kill thousands of Philistines. When the Philistine leaders learned that Samson loved Delilah, they offered her a huge amount of silver to find out the secret of his strength. Three times, Delilah asked Samson to reveal his secret, but Samson teased her by making up lies. Finally he admitted that he drew his strength from his long hair, which he had never cut. Delilah sent a message to the Philistine leaders, revealing Samson's secret.

CHAPTER 16 VERSE 23

"Our god has delivered Samson, our enemy, into our hands."

The Philistines believe that their god Dagon has allowed them to capture Samson. They hold a great festival to thank Dagon.

✛

CHAPTER 16 VERSE 28

"Please, God, strengthen me just once more..."

Samson prays to God to give him the strength to bring down Dagon's temple. His hair is a symbol of his strength, which really comes from God.

SAMSON'S HAIR IS CUT

After revealing his secret, Samson fell asleep in Delilah's lap and she quietly called for a servant to come into the room and cut off his long hair. The Philistines then rushed in and seized Samson, who had no strength to resist. They blinded him, and took him to a prison cell in Gaza.

The Philistine soldiers seize Samson.

Delilah has betrayed Samson for silver.

Samson brings the columns down, killing himself along with the Philistines.

Samson is in chains.

SAMSON'S REVENGE

Three thousand Philistines had gathered in the temple of the god Dagon, to celebrate Samson's capture. They brought Samson out of the prison to entertain them. Samson asked to be led between the pillars supporting the temple roof so he can lean against them. Samson prayed to God and shouted, "Let me die with the Philistines!" He then used all his strength to break the pillars, destroying the temple and killing everyone inside.

Delilah was **Samson's second** Philistine **wife**.

NAOMI AND RUTH

Ruth, Chapters 1–4

There was a woman called Naomi, who lived in Bethlehem with her husband Elimelek and their two sons. At the time, there was a famine in the land. To escape it, Elimelek took his family east, to Moab, where he died. Naomi's sons married two Moabite women, called Ruth and Orpah. But, after ten years of living in Moab, both of Naomi's sons also died. Naomi then learned that there was no longer a famine in her homeland, and she decided to leave Moab and go back to Bethlehem.

Ruth was the **great grandmother** of **David**, the future **king of Israel**.

CHAPTER 1 VERSE 15

"... *your sister-in-law is going back to her people and her gods.*"

Orpah stays with the people and gods of Moab. By going with Naomi, Ruth leaves not just her people but also the gods of her homeland.

Naomi's sons are buried in Moab.

RUTH FOLLOWS NAOMI

After the death of her sons, Naomi advised their widows to stay in Moab, and find new husbands. Orpah followed her advice, but Ruth begged to be taken along to Bethlehem. Ruth said that, "Your people will be my people, and your God my God." So the two women set off for Bethlehem.

Ruth   Orpah   Naomi

RUTH GLEANS

In Bethlehem, Ruth went to the barley fields to glean (gather stray grains left behind by the harvesters). The field belonged to Boaz, a relative of Naomi. He had heard of Ruth's loyalty to Naomi, and allowed Ruth to collect the grains left behind. He even ordered his workmen to drop grain in her path.

Boaz

Ruth

Ruth gathers stray grains of barley.

NAOMI'S ADVICE

Naomi saw that Boaz would make a good husband for Ruth. She knew that Boaz would be threshing (separating the grains from the husks) the harvested barley. So she told Ruth to wash, and then to lie at Boaz's feet while he slept on the threshing floor.

Ruth washes and perfumes herself.

Naomi

BOAZ AWAKES

Boaz woke in the night, and was startled to find a woman lying at his feet. She told him that she was Ruth, and that she had come to ask for his protection. Boaz said he would do all she asked. Later Ruth and Boaz married, and had a son called Obed.

Boaz wakes to see Ruth.

Ruth

ELI

1 Samuel, Chapters 1–6

Hannah brings Samuel to Eli.

Eli

SAMUEL

A childless woman called Hannah went to Shiloh, to pray for a son. After she gave birth, she named the child Samuel. When he grew up, Hannah took Samuel to Shiloh, to serve Eli in the tabernacle.

The **tabernacle** at Shiloh was later **destroyed** by the **Philistines**.

Samuel

During the time of the Judges, the city of Shiloh was the centre of Israelite worship. Here, the Ark of the Covenant, the box containing the Ten Commandments, was kept in a shrine called a tabernacle. The tabernacle was looked after by a High Priest. The last High Priest in Shiloh was a man called Eli. He was a good man, but his two sons, who were also priests, behaved wickedly. They would take offerings brought to God at the tabernacle for themselves. Eli was unable to control them. God told a boy called Samuel to tell Eli that he was going to punish the priest's sons.

SAMUEL WARNS ELI

When Samuel was sleeping in the tabernacle, God spoke to him, asking him to deliver a message to Eli. God said that Eli and his sons would shortly be punished. When Eli received this message, he replied sadly, "He is the Lord", accepting God's will.

THE PHILISTINES CAPTURE THE ARK

Soon after, the Israelites went to battle with the Philistines, taking the Ark of the Covenant with them. The Israelites suffered a terrible defeat. Both of Eli's sons were killed in the battle, and the Ark was captured by the Philistines.

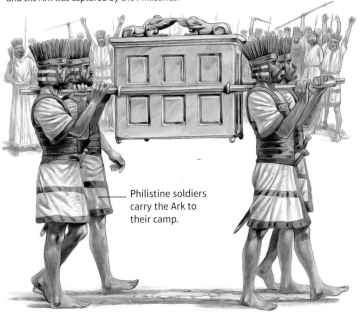

Philistine soldiers carry the Ark to their camp.

CHAPTER 3 VERSE 15
"He was afraid to tell Eli the vision..."
Samuel is afraid to pass on God's warning to Eli, but the High Priest tells Samuel not to hide anything from him.

CHAPTER 5 VERSE 11
"Send the ark of the god of Israel away..."
After the Philistines capture the Ark, they are struck with deadly swellings of the body wherever they take it. So they decide to send the Ark back to the Israelites.

HIGH PRIESTS

The High Priests were in charge of all Israelite religious ceremonies. They traced their family line back to Moses' brother, Aaron. The High Priests wore special clothes, including a breastplate set with twelve gemstones, each engraved with the name of one of the Twelve Tribes of Israel.

The messenger gives Eli the terrible news.

ELI'S DEATH

After the battle, a messenger ran back to Shiloh and told Eli that both his sons had been killed and the Ark had been taken by the Philistines. Eli was so shocked that he fell off his chair, broke his neck, and died.

75

SAMUEL

1 Samuel, Chapters 1-3, 8-10

While Samuel was still a child, his mother Hannah took him to Shiloh. She handed him over to Eli, the High Priest, saying that Samuel's life was to be dedicated to God. Samuel served in the tabernacle like the other priests. One night, while sleeping in the tabernacle, Samuel heard the voice of God, calling him to be a prophet. As he grew up, the Israelites saw that Samuel spoke for God, and they obeyed his judgements. Samuel was the last of the Judges and the greatest prophet since Moses.

The name **"Samuel"** means **"God hears"** in Hebrew.

SAMUEL IS CALLED

One night, Samuel was woken by a voice calling him by name. Samuel thought it was Eli, and ran to him. But Eli said it was not him, and told Samuel to go back to sleep. When Samuel heard the voice twice more, Eli realized that it was God speaking. He told Samuel to respond to the voice the next time. Samuel became God's prophet.

God tells Samuel to carry a message to Eli.

Samuel

Samuel

GOD'S WARNING

God told Samuel to warn the Israelites that a king would make their lives harsher. But, God said that if they still asked for a king, Samuel should agree to give them one.

THEY ASK FOR A KING

When Samuel grew old, the elders of Israel, who had relied on his leadership, worried about who would lead them after his death. So they asked him to choose a king to rule over them. This displeased Samuel, who thought only God could be king.

CHAPTER 8 VERSE 20

"... we will be like all the other nations, with a king to lead us..."

Despite Samuel's warnings about life under a king, the Israelites still want a ruler. They need a powerful leader to protect them from the Philistines, who are once more threatening Israel.

Samuel anoints the young Saul, making him king.

SAMUEL ANOINTS SAUL

God led Samuel to a tall and handsome young man called Saul, from the tribe of Benjamin. God told Samuel to make Saul the king of Israel, by anointing him (pouring oil over his head). So Saul became the first king of Israel.

Saul

SAUL
1 Samuel, Chapters 15, 28–31

Samuel

Saul grabs
Samuel's robe
to stop him
from leaving.

SAMUEL'S ROBE

Saul won a battle against the Amalekites. But Samuel told him that despite his victory, God still rejected him as king. As Samuel turned to leave, Saul grabbed his robe and tore it. Samuel explained that God had torn the kingdom of Israel from Saul, to give to a better man.

Saul, the first king of Israel, was a brave warrior, who won many battles against Israel's enemies. After defeating the Ammonites, he planned to lead the Israelites against the Philistines. But he could not go into battle before making an offering to God. The prophet Samuel told Saul to wait until he arrived to make the offering. After waiting a week for Samuel, Saul lost his patience, and made the offering himself. When Samuel arrived, he told Saul that, by disobeying his orders, Saul had lost God's favour. God would now find a better man to be anointed as king.

CHAPTER 15 VERSE 28

"... to one better than you."

Samuel tells Saul that because of his disobedience, God will choose a better man to be king. The better man is David, a shepherd boy from Bethlehem, who will be Israel's next ruler.

The witch calls up the spirit of Samuel.

THE SPIRIT OF SAMUEL

After Samuel died, Saul wanted to speak to the dead man's spirit, to learn more about his own fate. So he went to a witch, in Endor, who could call up spirits. The witch raised Samuel, who told Saul he would die at the hands of the Philistines the very next day.

Samuel is angry with Saul for disturbing his rest.

Saul defied the **Law of Moses**, which **forbade** the **raising** of **spirits**.

Many Israelites die in the battle.

Saul kills himself.

THE DEATH OF SAUL

The next day, just as Samuel foretold, the Philistines attacked and defeated Saul and his army. Many Israelites, including three of Saul's sons, were killed. Saul was badly wounded with an arrow, and could not escape. But rather than allow himself to be captured, Saul stabbed himself in the belly with his sword.

Samuel

David

DAVID
1 Samuel, Chapters 16–20; **2 Samuel**, Chapters 5–6

David, son of Jesse, was a shepherd boy from Bethlehem. God had chosen David to succeed Saul as the king of Israel. While he was still a boy, David killed a giant Philistine called Goliath. King Saul then made David an army commander. Whenever Saul sent David into battle he was victorious, killing tens of thousands of Philistines. David's victories made Saul so jealous that he tried to kill him. David fled to the wilderness, where he lived as an outlaw. After Saul and his sons were killed in battle, the Israelites needed a new ruler. Remembering David's victories over the Philistines, they asked him to be their king.

DAVID ANOINTED
God asked the prophet Samuel to go to Bethlehem, where he would find a son of Jesse to anoint as the next king. Samuel looked at all eight sons of Jesse and it was David, the youngest, who was chosen by God. Samuel anointed David with oil and from then on God was with him.

Saul tries to kill David with his spear.

The spear just misses David.

SAUL TRIES TO KILL DAVID
Later, when David had become a successful commander in Saul's army, the king became jealous of his victories. One day, while David was playing a harp to soothe the king, Saul threw a spear at him. David narrowly escaped.

1 SAMUEL
CHAPTER 18 VERSE 12

"... the Lord was with David but had departed from Saul."

Saul has dark moods because he knows that he has lost God's favour. He sees that God now favours David, and so he fears him and tries to kill him.

CITY OF DAVID

David's greatest success was the capture of Jerusalem, a very old hill town, which he made his royal capital. He brought the Ark of the Covenant there, making the city a centre for Israelite religious worship. Jerusalem is still known as the City of David.

CAPTURING JERUSALEM

After Saul's death, David became king. He and his army marched to Jerusalem, a town which was home to the Jebusites. The Jebusites boasted that nobody could capture Jerusalem because of its strong walls. But David used a water shaft to get into the city and his army conquered Jerusalem.

Joab is David's chief army commander.

Jerusalem was a **natural stronghold**, protected by **valleys** on **three sides**.

David tells Joab how to capture Jerusalem.

The Old Testament

81

GOLIATH'S CHALLENGE

For forty days, Goliath shouted his challenge. He said that if an Israelite could kill him, the Philistines would become their servants. But if Goliath won, the Israelites would have to serve the Philistines. The Israelites were all too scared of Goliath to offer to fight him, until David arrived.

Goliath wears a massive suit of bronze armour.

DAVID AND GOLIATH
1 Samuel, Chapter 17

The Philistines gathered a large army, and came to attack the Israelites. They camped on a hill overlooking the Valley of Elah. King Saul and the Israelite army camped on a hill on the other side. A champion warrior, called Goliath, then came out of the Philistine camp. He stood more than three metres tall and wore a suit of bronze armour. Goliath challenged the Israelites to send out a champion of their own to fight him. Nobody from the Israelite camp was willing to fight him, until David, the shepherd boy from Bethlehem, came forward and asked Saul to let him fight Goliath.

SLING AND STONES

A sling was a leather pad with a cord on either side. The slinger put a stone on the pad, and holding the cords, whirled it around his head, letting go of one cord to launch the stone. It was used by shepherds, such as David, to protect their flocks from wolves.

DAVID FIGHTS GOLIATH

Goliath could not believe his eyes when he saw that the Israelites had sent a boy to fight him. But then David put a large stone in his sling, and let it fly straight at the giant. It hit him in the middle of his forehead, and he crashed to the ground. When the Philistines saw Goliath was dead, they ran away.

The stone hits Goliath square between the eyes.

David

David faced Goliath with just his **sling and five stones**.

Goliath

JONATHAN

1 Samuel, Chapters 13-14, 18-20, 23; **2 Samuel**, Chapter 1

Jonathan was King Saul's son, and David's dearest friend. As the king's son, he could expect to rule after Saul. But Jonathan knew that God had chosen David to rule. Jonathan made a solemn oath of loyalty to David. When Saul told his son that he wanted to kill David, Jonathan warned his friend and helped David escape. David loved Jonathan in return. When he learned that Jonathan had been killed fighting the Philistines, he wept for him. David made a famous lament, a song of sorrow, in which he sang, "How the mighty have fallen!"

Michal, Jonathan's sister, was **married to David**.

JONATHAN THE WARRIOR
Jonathan always put his trust in God to bring him victory. During one battle, when he had only his armour bearer (a servant who carried weapons) with him, he attacked and killed twenty Philistines. God then made the Philistine army panic and run away.

Jonathan charges at a much bigger Philistine force.

Jonathan's armour bearer

Jonathan

David

Saul

JONATHAN SWEARS LOYALTY

When David was hiding from Saul, Jonathan went to see him. He told David not to be afraid, as God would protect him. He renewed his covenant with David, and said, "You shall be king over Israel, and I will be second to you. Even my father Saul knows this."

SAUL'S WARNING

When Saul came to fear David as a rival he expected Jonathan to feel the same way. He warned his son that, as long as David lived, Jonathan would never be king. However, Saul did not know that Jonathan had accepted that David would be the next king.

Jonathan tells David he will be king.

David

1 SAMUEL CHAPTER 18 VERSE 3

"... Jonathan made a covenant with David..."

Jonathan makes a covenant, a solemn promise to David that he will always serve him. He gives David his robe and weapons as a sign of the covenant.

1 SAMUEL CHAPTER 20 VERSE 30

"Saul's anger flared up at Jonathan..."

Saul can't understand why his son protects David, who threatens his own chance of becoming king. Jonathan cares more about God's will than being king.

BATHSHEBA
2 Samuel, Chapters 11-12

David falls in love with Bathsheba.

David

Bathsheba

Bathsheba was the beautiful wife of Uriah, one of David's most loyal soldiers. One day, from the roof of his palace, David saw Bathsheba bathing and was struck by her beauty. He sent for Bathsheba and they slept together. Bathsheba later told David that they would have a baby. At the time, David's army was fighting a war against the Ammonites. To get rid of Uriah, who was fighting in his army, David ordered his commander to send Uriah to the frontline of the battle, where the fighting was fiercest. Uriah was killed, and David took Bathsheba for his wife.

DAVID IS PUNISHED

Bathsheba gave birth to a boy. But God was angry with David for stealing Uriah's wife and arranging his death. He sent a prophet called Nathan to tell David that he would be punished, and that his newborn son would die. A week later, the boy died, just as Nathan foretold.

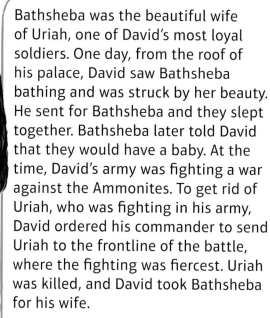

Bathsheba and David had a **second son – Solomon**, the future king of Israel.

ABSALOM
2 Samuel, Chapters 13-18

Absalom's death fulfills **Nathan's prophecy** that David would **be punished**.

Absalom

Joab prepares to kill Absalom with his javelins.

Joab

CAUGHT BY THE HAIR

While escaping from David's army on his mule, Absalom's long hair became caught in the branches of an oak tree. He was left dangling in mid-air. Here Joab, one of David's commanders, found Absalom and killed him.

David had a son called Absalom, who was handsome and popular with the people. Although David loved him dearly, Absalom plotted to take his father's crown. He gathered many followers, proclaimed himself king, and challenged his father to battle. David gave orders to prepare for battle, but asked his commanders to be gentle with Absalom. The battle was a terrible defeat for Absalom, who escaped by riding away on a mule but then was captured and killed.

CHAPTER 18 VERSE 33

"My son, my son Absalom! If only I had died instead of you..."
David mourns the death of his son deeply. By killing Absalom, Joab has disobeyed David's order to be gentle with him.

NATHAN
1 Kings, Chapter 1

Nathan was the chief prophet during David's reign, and was not afraid to tell the king when he did wrong. As Nathan foretold, David was punished for taking Bathsheba, and his reign ended in many troubles. When David grew old and neared death, there was a struggle over who would rule next. His older son, Adonijah, began behaving as if he was king, without even asking his father's permission. But David had already promised Bathsheba that Solomon, their young son, would rule after him. Nathan believed that Solomon, not Adonijah, was God's choice to be king of Israel.

CHAPTER 1 VERSE 30
"... Solomon your son shall be king after me..."
David swears a solemn oath to Bathsheba to keep his promise to her. Although David is old and weak, he shows his energy and forcefulness here.

DAVID'S PROMISE
Nathan and Bathsheba told David that Adonijah had declared himself king. Nathan urged David to keep his promise so that Solomon would rule after him. David, who trusted Nathan's advice, swore that he would make Solomon king.

Abishag, David's carer

David

Nathan

Bathsheba

SOLOMON

1 Kings, Chapter 1

»»

Solomon was still a boy when he was proclaimed king on David's orders. Nathan and Zadok the priest took young Solomon to the spring of Gihon, outside the walls of Jerusalem. Here, Zadok anointed Solomon with oil. Then they sounded trumpets, and all the people shouted, "Long live King Solomon!" David's older son Adonijah, who was at a feast, heard the noise and asked what was going on. When he was told that Solomon had just been anointed, Adonijah immediately gave up his claim to be king. He begged Solomon not to kill him, and Solomon pardoned him.

GOD'S ANOINTED

Solomon knelt on the ground, while Zadok poured oil over his head. With this holy ceremony, Solomon became king of Israel. He was supported by both the priest and the prophet, which showed that he was God's choice to rule.

The commander of the palace guard watches over the ceremony.

Nathan

Zadok

Solomon

SOLOMON'S TEMPLE
1 Kings, Chapters 5–8

After years of warfare, King Solomon's reign was a time of peace for Israel. So the king decided to build a great temple in Jerusalem, which his father, David, had longed to build as a place of worship. It took seven years to build the temple. When finally completed, the priests brought in the Ark of the Covenant and placed it in the inner room. After they withdrew, a great cloud suddenly appeared from nowhere, filling the building. This was a sign that God had arrived, to take his place in Solomon's temple.

Unlike other ancient temples, **Solomon's temple had no statue of a god**.

Sculptors use hammers and chisels to carve decorations.

BUILDING THE TEMPLE
Solomon's friend, King Hiram of Tyre (in modern-day Lebanon) helped in the building of the temple by sending workmen, and cedar wood from the forests of his kingdom. In the quarries above Jerusalem, large stones were shaped into blocks, to build walls. At the building site, sculptors carved images of cherubim (winged heavenly creatures) and flowers into the blocks to decorate the temple.

An overseer inspects the sculptor's work.

Two large columns, called Jakin and Boaz, are built in front of the entrance.

Solomon oversees the building of the temple, which followed David's plan.

The large stone blocks are moved with the help of oxen.

INSIDE THE TEMPLE

Inside the temple was a big hall called the Holy Place. Behind it was a smaller room, called the Holy of Holies, which housed the Ark of the Covenant. This was the most sacred part of the temple.

The Holy of Holies

Solomon

THE QUEEN OF SHEBA

1 Kings, Chapters 4, 10

Solomon was wiser than any other person on earth. His fame spread to all the surrounding nations, and many foreigners came to visit him. When the Queen of Sheba heard about his wealth and wisdom, she could not believe the stories. To find out if they were true, and to test Solomon's wisdom, the queen travelled all the way to Jerusalem. When she arrived, Solomon gave her a warm welcome, and then he showed her around his beautiful palace. She was impressed by the wealth of his court, but more so by his wisdom.

Sheba was in south-west Arabia, a place now in **Yemen**.

TO JERUSALEM

To reach Jerusalem, the queen had to travel 2,200 km (1,400 miles) north, across the deserts of Arabia. She took with her a great caravan of camels, loaded with spices, gold, and precious stones – all gifts for Solomon.

The Queen of Sheba

Solomon

The queen brings chests full of gold vessels and other gifts for Solomon.

TESTING SOLOMON

To test Solomon, the queen asked him many difficult questions. He easily answered them, and the queen was amazed at the wisdom of his replies. She told Solomon that although she had thought the stories of his wisdom could not be true, he was even wiser than she had been told.

CHAPTER 4 VERSE 29

"God gave Solomon wisdom..."
Solomon's great wisdom is described as a gift from God. It is a sign that God favours Israel.

✣

CHAPTER 10 VERSE 9

"Because of the Lord's eternal love for Israel, he has made you king..."
The Queen of Sheba recognizes that God has blessed Israel by making such a wise man king.

TRADING IN SHEBA

Sheba's wealth came from its trees, which produced frankincense and myrrh. These sweet smelling resins were used to make perfume and burned as offerings in temples. Merchants from Sheba sailed east to India, where they traded these resins for spices, such as cinnamon.

Cinnamon

Frankincense

Myrrh

REHOBOAM

1 Kings, Chapters 12-13

After Solomon died, his son Rehoboam became king of Israel. The northern tribes had been unhappy under Solomon's rule, because he taxed them heavily and forced them to work on his building projects. Their spokesman, Jeroboam, told Rehoboam that if he made their lives easier, they would serve him loyally. But Rehoboam said that his rule would be even harsher than his father's. At this, the ten northern tribes refused to have him as their king. Only the two southern tribes of Judah and Benjamin stayed loyal to Rehoboam. The kingdom was now divided in two, Judah in the south, and Israel in the north.

CHAPTER 12 VERSE 1

"Rehoboam went to Shechem..."

Rehoboam's meeting with Jeroboam is in Shechem, a holy place, where Abraham built the first altar, by the tree of Moreh.

CHAPTER 12 VERSE 14

"My father made your yoke heavy..."

A yoke is a crosspiece carried by oxen pulling a plough or cart. The yoke here means hard work and taxes imposed by the King Solomon, which Rehoboam wishes to continue.

MEETING JEROBOAM

Rehoboam's older advisers told him to agree to Jeroboam's request. But Rehoboam preferred the advice of his young friends, who told him to rule firmly.

Rehoboam tells Jeroboam he plans to rule harshly.

JEROBOAM
1 Kings, Chapters 12-13

JEROBOAM'S HAND
The man of God said that the altar would split as a sign that his prophecy was God's will. Angered at this, Jeroboam pointed at the man and cried, "Seize him!" His hand suddenly shrivelled up and the altar split apart. Jeroboam begged the man to ask God to restore his hand. So the man prayed, and Jeroboam's hand was healed.

Jeroboam's hand shrivels up.

The man of God prays for Jeroboam's hand to be healed.

Jeroboam

The altar is split apart.

After the ten tribes broke away from Rehoboam's rule, Jeroboam was made king of the northern kingdom of Israel. But he was afraid he would lose his kingdom if people continued to worship in Solomon's temple in Judah. So he had two golden calves made, and set up altars for them in Bethel and Dan, at each end of his kingdom. A man of God from Judah came to the altar in Bethel, where he was shocked to see Jeroboam worshipping a golden calf. He told Jeroboam that one day, a king called Josiah would destroy this altar.

CHAPTER 13 VERSE 2
"A son named Josiah..."
The prophecy made by the man of God comes true when Josiah, who ruled the southern kingdom of Judah from 640–609 BCE, destroys the altar at Bethel.

AHAB AND JEZEBEL

1 Kings, Chapters 16-17, 21

Ahab was the eighth king of the northern kingdom of Israel, which he ruled from Samaria, his capital. Ahab married Jezebel, a Phoenician princess who was the daughter of the King of Sidon. Ahab was so influenced by Jezebel that he built a temple to her god, Baal, in Samaria. The prophet Elijah warned Ahab that Israel would suffer a drought as punishment for building temples to other gods. And there was a drought, which lasted for three years. It ended after Elijah won a contest against the prophets of Baal, to see whose god was more powerful. Elijah then caused the rain to fall once more on Israel.

CHAPTER 17 VERSE 1

"... there will be neither dew nor rain..."

Baal was worshipped as a weather god, bringing rain. By withholding rain, God is shown to be more powerful than Baal.

JEZEBEL AND NABOTH'S VINEYARD

Ahab wanted a vineyard owned by a man called Naboth. When Naboth refused to sell it to him, Ahab lay on his bed, sulking and refusing to eat. Jezebel said, "Is this how you act as king over Israel?" She then said that she would get Naboth's vineyard for him.

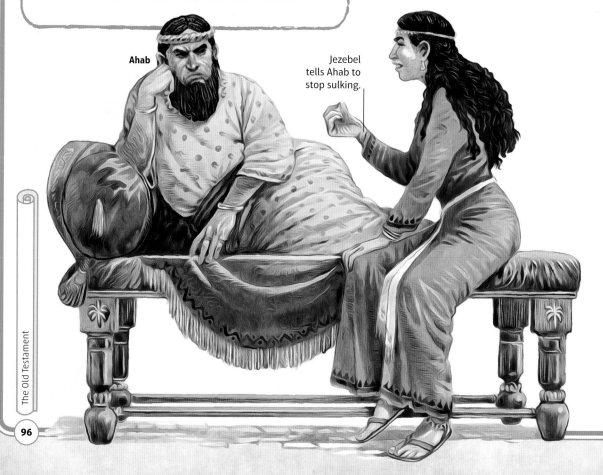

Ahab

Jezebel tells Ahab to stop sulking.

FALSE ACCUSATIONS
Jezebel wrote letters in Ahab's name, calling the leading men of Naboth's city to a meeting. There she had two men falsely accuse Naboth of cursing God. For this, Naboth was stoned to death. Jezebel then told Ahab that he could take possession of the vineyard.

BAAL
The word Baal means "Lord" and is a title rather than the name of a particular god. The names of gods were thought to be too holy to be spoken aloud by their worshippers. The "Baal" worshipped by Jezebel and Ahab is likely to have been Melqart, who was the chief god of Sidon. This statue shows one of several gods called Baal.

Under the Law of Moses, **cursing God** was **punishable by death**.

ELIJAH'S WARNING
Ahab was delighted to get hold of Naboth's vineyard. But Elijah told Ahab and Jezebel that they were guilty of murdering a man and stealing his property. Elijah said that, because of their crime, disaster would fall upon them, and Ahab's kingdom would be destroyed.

Elijah warns Ahab and Jezebel.

Ahab is horrified at Elijah's words.

ELIJAH

1 Kings, Chapter 18 ; **2 Kings**, Chapter 2

Elijah has the prophets of Baal killed.

Elijah

ELIJAH'S ALTAR

Elijah stood in front of his altar, and prayed to God three times. In answer to his prayer, a flame leapt up from the altar. At this, everybody fell to the ground shouting, "The Lord – he is God!" Ahab galloped away in his chariot, back to Jezreel. But Elijah outran him, and got there first.

Elijah runs ahead of Ahab's chariot back to Jezreel.

God sent the prophet Elijah to see King Ahab, a follower of Baal. Elijah went to Ahab's palace in Jezreel and challenged Ahab to send the prophets of Baal to meet him on Mount Carmel. There they would hold a contest to see whose god was more powerful. So Ahab, as well as four hundred and fifty prophets, went to Mount Carmel. The prophets danced around an altar to Baal from morning until noon, calling on Baal to show his power by lighting the altar on fire. But there was no answer from Baal. When it was Elijah's turn, the altar he had built to God burst into flames.

The city of Jezreel is about **40 km** (25 miles) away **from Mount Carmel**.

Elisha is amazed when Elijah parts the river with his cloak.

CARRIED INTO HEAVEN
Elijah asked Elisha if he had a last request. Elisha replied that he wanted to inherit Elijah's role as God's prophet. Elijah said that if Elisha saw him carried into heaven, it would show that his wish had been granted. Elijah was then carried into heaven by a whirlwind in front of Elisha's eyes.

Elisha

Elijah

Elisha asks Elijah if he can be a prophet like him.

ELIJAH AND ELISHA
Elijah had a loyal follower called Elisha, who followed him wherever he went. When Elijah grew very old, he knew that God would soon take him up into heaven. Elijah told Elisha to stay behind while he went to the River Jordan. Elisha refused to leave him. When they reached the river, Elijah parted its water with his cloak, and they walked across on dry land.

Elijah rides the whirlwind to heaven in a chariot of fire.

Elisha sees Elijah being taken away.

The Old Testament

ELISHA

2 Kings, Chapters 2–5

Elisha uses Elijah's cloak to part the river.

Elisha

After he saw Elijah carried into heaven, Elisha inherited his power as God's prophet. He became well known throughout Israel as a holy man. News of Elisha's ability to work miracles reached even the kingdom of Aram, north of Israel. Naaman, commander of the Aram army, was a brave and successful warrior, but he was sick with leprosy. His wife had an Israelite slave girl who suggested that he visit Elisha to be cured. So Naaman rode his chariot to Elisha's house in Israel.

ELIJAH'S CLOAK

Elisha performed many miracles. The first miracle was to part the River Jordan, using the cloak which Elijah had dropped to the ground. When Elisha struck the river with it, the waters divided and he walked across to the other side.

Naaman hides his sickness by keeping himself covered.

NAAMAN VISITS ELISHA

When Naaman arrived at Elisha's house, Elisha sent out a servant, who told him to wash himself seven times in the River Jordan in order to be cured. Naaman, a proud man, was angry that Elisha hadn't come to meet him and had sent a servant. But Naaman's own servants persuaded him to try Elisha's cure.

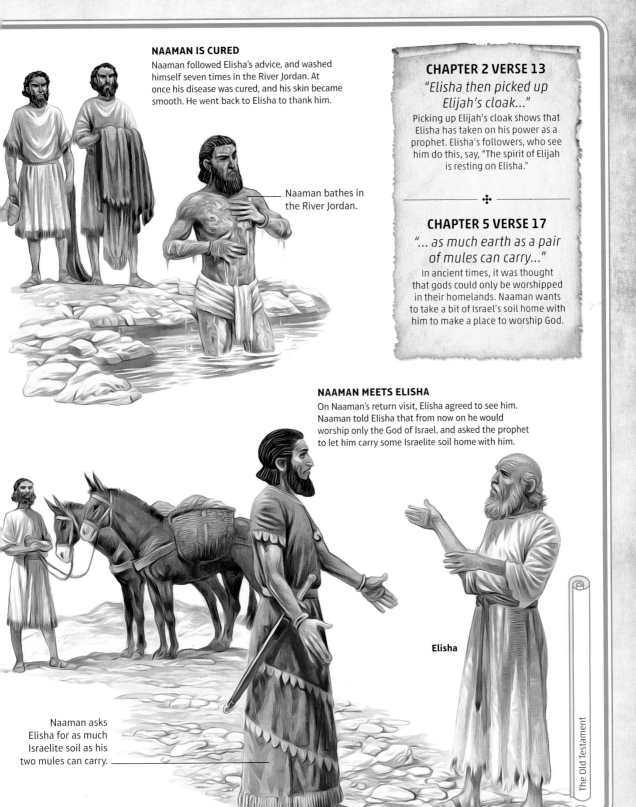

NAAMAN IS CURED

Naaman followed Elisha's advice, and washed himself seven times in the River Jordan. At once his disease was cured, and his skin became smooth. He went back to Elisha to thank him.

Naaman bathes in the River Jordan.

CHAPTER 2 VERSE 13

"Elisha then picked up Elijah's cloak..."

Picking up Elijah's cloak shows that Elisha has taken on his power as a prophet. Elisha's followers, who see him do this, say, "The spirit of Elijah is resting on Elisha."

⸬

CHAPTER 5 VERSE 17

"... as much earth as a pair of mules can carry..."

In ancient times, it was thought that gods could only be worshipped in their homelands. Naaman wants to take a bit of Israel's soil home with him to make a place to worship God.

NAAMAN MEETS ELISHA

On Naaman's return visit, Elisha agreed to see him. Naaman told Elisha that from now on he would worship only the God of Israel, and asked the prophet to let him carry some Israelite soil home with him.

Elisha

Naaman asks Elisha for as much Israelite soil as his two mules can carry.

JONAH

Jonah, Chapters 1–4

One of God's prophets, Jonah, lived in the kingdom of Israel during the reign of Jeroboam II. One day, God told Jonah to go to Nineveh, and warn the people that their city would be destroyed if they did not give up their wicked ways. But Jonah disobeyed and ran in the opposite direction from Nineveh. He went to the port of Joppa and found a ship sailing east. God, angry with Jonah, sent a storm that almost destroyed the ship. The terrified sailors drew lots to find out whom to blame for the storm, and they found that it was Jonah. He admitted that the storm was his fault, and asked to be thrown overboard.

"Jonah" is a Hebrew name **meaning "dove"**.

When the sailors throw Jonah overboard, the storm is calmed at once.

A GREAT FISH
After the sailors threw Jonah overboard, the raging sea instantly grew calm. Jonah expected to drown, but God sent a huge fish to swallow him. He ended up in the creature's belly, where he spent three days and three nights, praying to God to forgive him. Jonah said, "Salvation comes from the Lord!"

CHAPTER 1 VERSE 3

"... Jonah ran away from the Lord..."

Jonah runs away because he wants God to destroy Nineveh. This was because the Ninevites were enemies of the Israelites.

✛

CHAPTER 1 VERSE 7

"They cast lots and the lot fell on Jonah."

The custom of casting lots is mentioned seventy-seven times in the Bible, but we do not know how it was done. It may have been by drawing straws of different lengths.

WHALES

Although the Bible calls the creature that swallowed Jonah "a huge fish", it is usually thought to be a whale. There are stories of people who have survived after being swallowed by sperm whales, and then spat out.

THE VINE TREE

After leaving Nineveh, Jonah took shelter under the shade of a vine. God caused the vine to shrivel up, angering Jonah. God then told Jonah that he was wrong to care more about the vine than he did about the people of Nineveh.

SPAT OUT

Hearing Jonah's prayer, God commanded the great fish to release him, and it spat Jonah out onto dry land. Jonah then went to Nineveh, where his preaching made the people turn away from their past wickedness. Because of this, God did not destroy the city. Jonah became angry that God had spared Nineveh.

AHAZ
2 Chronicles, Chapter 28

Ahaz

Ahaz, who became the king of Judah when he was twenty years old, worshipped idols, setting up statues of Baal and other gods. To punish him for this, God allowed Ahaz to be defeated in war by the kings of Israel and Aram. Ahaz asked King Tiglath-Pileser of Assyria for help against these enemies. The Assyrian king agreed but at a price. To pay for his protection, Ahaz had to send a large amount of treasure to the Assyrians, which he took from the temple. Ahaz would later be remembered as the worst king to rule Judah.

CHILD SACRIFICE
Ahaz worshipped the old Canaanite gods, such as Baal, as well as the gods of Aram and Assyria. He even sacrificed his own children to these gods, burning their bones on the altars.

Soldiers strip the temple of its treasures.

Temple furnishings are taken to be cut into pieces.

CLOSING THE TEMPLE
Ahaz closed the temple in Jerusalem, which had been built by Solomon, and he had its furnishings cut into pieces. He used the treasures from the temple to pay the Assyrians for their protection. He then set up altars to foreign gods on every street corner in the city.

CHAPTER 28 VERSE 27
"... he was not placed in the tombs of the kings of Israel."
Ahaz was so hated by the people that he was not buried in the royal tombs of Jerusalem, alongside the other kings.

ISAIAH AND HEZEKIAH

Isaiah, Chapters 36–39

Isaiah was a prophet who lived in Jerusalem, in Judah, during the reign of King Hezekiah, son of Ahaz. Hezekiah was a good king, who reopened the temple and destroyed the shrines set up by his father. At the time, the Assyrians had conquered Israel. They invaded Judah, and captured every city except Jerusalem. With the Assyrian army surrounding Jerusalem, Hezekiah went into the temple to pray, and then sent for Isaiah. The prophet told the king not to be afraid, for the Assyrians would not enter the holy city. The next day, God struck the Assyrian army with a plague, and the Assyrian king, Sennacherib, fled home to Nineveh.

CHAPTER 38 VERSE 5

"I have heard your prayer..."
God asks Isaiah to tell Hezekiah that, because he has been a good king, he will be healed. God adds fifteen years to his life.

HEZEKIAH'S ILLNESS

Straight after the victory over the Assyrians, Hezekiah fell seriously ill, and everyone expected him to die. But he prayed hard for healing. Isaiah told the king's servants to treat him with a mixture of figs, and Hezekiah's health improved.

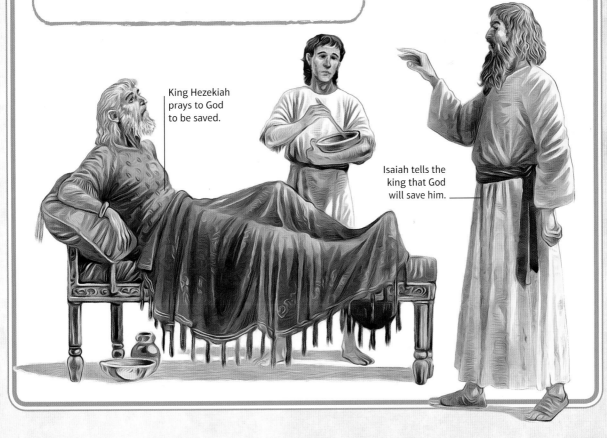

King Hezekiah prays to God to be saved.

Isaiah tells the king that God will save him.

JOSIAH

2 Chronicles, Chapters 34–35

Josiah

A priest throws the bones of an idol worshipper onto the altar.

After Hezekiah's death, the kingdom of Judah was ruled by two kings who worshipped foreign gods. Then Josiah, Hezekiah's great-grandson, became king at just eight years old. When Josiah was sixteen, he decided to restore the worship of God. He destroyed all the pagan altars and had the temple in Jerusalem, which had fallen into ruins, restored. While the temple was being repaired, the High Priest, Hilkiah, found an ancient scroll there. It was the Book of the Law of Moses.

DESTROYING THE ALTARS

Josiah wanted to get rid of any trace of idol worship. So he had the bones of the priests who had worshipped foreign gods dug up and burnt on the pagan altars. He then tore down these altars and scattered their stones.

CHAPTER 34 VERSE 14

"... the Book of the Law..."

We do not know if the High Priest found all five books of Moses, which were thought to be lost. This "book" may refer to the fifth book, called Deuteronomy. It contains sermons given by Moses to the Israelites before they entered Canaan.

JOSIAH READS THE LAW

After the temple was restored, Josiah called all the people of Jerusalem to assemble there. He then read out the book that Hilkiah had found, and made a solemn promise to follow God's laws.

JEREMIAH

Jeremiah, Chapters 1, 19

In the thirteenth year of Josiah's reign, God called a young man called Jeremiah to be his prophet. As a prophet, Jeremiah repeatedly warned that the kingdom of Judah faced destruction, as punishment for failing to obey God's laws. He served as a prophet for forty years, giving his warnings to the last five kings of Judah. At the end of his life, Jeremiah saw his prophecies come true. Jerusalem was captured by King Nebuchadnezzar of Babylon, who destroyed the temple, and took the people of Judah to Babylon as his prisoners. Jeremiah then composed poems in which he wept over the fall of the city.

CHAPTER 1 VERSE 6

"I do not know how to speak..."
When Jeremiah is first called to be a prophet, he says he is too young. God tells him not to be afraid.

✛

CHAPTER 1 VERSE 13

"I see a pot that is boiling..."
Jeremiah has a vision of a boiling pot, tilting towards Judah from the north. This pot represents the armies of Babylon, which will pour destruction on Judah from the north.

THE CLAY POT

Jeremiah bought a clay pot, and smashed it on the ground in front of the people of Judah. He told them that if they did not change their ways, God would destroy Judah, in just the way Jeremiah had smashed the pot.

Jeremiah smashes the clay pot.

The Old Testament

EZEKIEL

Ezekiel, Chapters 1–11

After King Nebuchadnezzar captured Jerusalem, he took the leading Jewish people away with him to Babylon. Among them was Ezekiel, a priest. In Babylon, Ezekiel was standing by the river when he saw the heavens open and he had visions of God. He saw a great storm cloud, and in the centre were four heavenly beings. Above them was something that seemed like a man on a throne, gleaming brightly. It was God, calling Ezekiel to be his prophet. God told Ezekiel to warn the people that Jerusalem would be destroyed. It was the first of many visions that Ezekiel had in his lifetime.

GOD'S WARNING

In his vision, God carried Ezekiel to the temple in Jerusalem, where he saw that the Jews who had stayed behind were now worshipping idols. God told Ezekiel that the temple and the city would be destroyed as a punishment.

CHAPTER 10 VERSE 18

"Then the glory of the lord departed..."

Ezekiel sees God abandoning the temple in Jerusalem. Nebuchadnezzar destroyed the temple in 586 BCE, following a Jewish uprising.

✠

CHAPTER 11 VERSE 17

"... I will give you back the land of Israel again."

God offers hope to Ezekiel. He promises that if the exiles in Babylon keep his laws, he will let them return one day to the Promised Land.

NEBUCHADNEZZAR

Daniel, Chapter 3

Nebuchadnezzar was the King of Babylon, who captured Jerusalem and later destroyed the city. He set up a great golden statue to one of Babylon's pagan gods, and told the chief officials of his kingdom to worship it. Three of the officials, called Shadrach, Meshach, and Abednego, were Jewish and refused. Nebuchadnezzar threatened to throw them into a blazing furnace if they did not worship the statue. The three men said that God would protect them from the furnace, and even if God did not, they would never worship a statue. So the king had them tied up and thrown into the furnace.

CHAPTER 3 VERSE 28

"Praise be to the God..."
Nebuchadnezzar is so impressed when he sees that the three Jews have survived the furnace that he praises the God who protected them.

IN THE FURNACE

Later Nebuchadnezzar looked into the furnace, which had been heated seven times hotter than usual. He was amazed to see the three Jews walking around, untied and unharmed. Beside them was a fourth man, who looked like a heavenly being. It was an angel, sent by God to protect them.

Nebuchadnezzar sees that the men are unharmed.

An angel appears beside the three men.

DANIEL

Daniel, Chapters 1–2

Daniel was a high-ranking captive from Judah, who was brought to Babylon as a prisoner by King Nebuchadnezzar. Daniel was chosen to serve as a royal official, along with some other Jewish nobles. One night, Nebuchadnezzar had a bad dream, which disturbed him greatly. He summoned all the wisest men of his court and asked them to describe his dream and explain what it meant. If they failed to do so, he would have them cut into pieces. Daniel had a special gift – he could interpret dreams. When he heard about the king's order, he offered to describe the dream and interpret it.

CHAPTER 2 VERSE 39

"... another kingdom will arise..."

The statue in the dream represents a series of empires, perhaps Babylon (gold), Persia (silver), Greece (bronze), and Rome (iron).

✢

CHAPTER 2 VERSE 44

"It will crush all those kingdoms..."

The rock that smashes the statue represents the rule of God. Daniel says that in the future, God will end earthly empires such as that of Nebuchadnezzar's.

THE WISE MEN

The wise men told Nebuchadnezzar that there was not a man on earth who could describe his dream. The king was so angry that he ordered all the wise men in Babylon to be put to death.

The wise men cannot explain the king's dream.

Nebuchadnezzar is troubled by his dream.

Nebuchadnezzar

The statue is shattered by a rock.

Daniel sees the king's dream in a vision.

Daniel

THE KING'S DREAM
During the night, Daniel had a vision from God, showing him the king's dream. The next day, Daniel told the king that he had seen a statue with a gold head, a silver chest, bronze thighs, and feet of iron and clay. A rock struck the statue, breaking it apart.

In **Hebrew**, the name "Daniel" means **"God is my judge"**.

Daniel offers to explain the king's dreams to him.

Nebuchadnezzar, amazed by Daniel's explanation, falls to his knees before Daniel.

EXPLAINING THE DREAM
Daniel explained to Nebuchadnezzar that the statue's gold head stood for the king himself. Its silver chest represented a lesser kingdom that would follow his own. This would be followed by a third kingdom, of bronze, which would rule the earth. Finally, there would be a fourth kingdom, strong as iron. The rock that destroyed the statue was the kingdom of God that would be everlasting.

DANIEL IN THE LIONS' DEN
Daniel, Chapter 6

In later years, when Darius became king of Babylon, he made Daniel one of his chief governors. Daniel proved to be such a good governor that Darius planned to put him in charge of the whole kingdom. This made the other officials jealous, and they plotted against Daniel. They persuaded the king to issue a decree, according to which anyone caught praying to any god or man except to Darius, during the next thirty days, would be thrown into the lions' den. The officials knew that Daniel prayed to God three times a day, and that no royal decree would stop him.

TRICKING THE KING
When the officials found Daniel praying as usual, despite the king's decree, they went and told Darius. The king was very upset, for he did not want to harm Daniel. But they reminded the king that no royal decree could be disobeyed.

Daniel prays to God. ———

THROWN TO THE LIONS
The king gave the order and Daniel was thrown into the lions' den. Darius was so worried about Daniel that he spent the whole night without sleep. The next morning, he hurried to the lions' den, and found that Daniel was unharmed. God had protected Daniel from the lions.

The officials who tricked the king are taken to the lions.

When the **Bible** was written, **wild lions** still lived in the **Middle East**.

DANIEL IS RELEASED

Darius, overjoyed to find Daniel safe, had him released. The king punished the officials who had tricked him by having them thrown to the same lions. As soon as they entered the den, the lions killed them. Darius then issued a new decree, honouring the God who had protected Daniel.

The lions do not harm Daniel.

LIONS OF BABYLON

Because of its strength, the lion was seen as a symbol of royal power. Babylonian kings also showed their strength by hunting lions. Using a bow and arrow, they hunted the lions from chariots. One of the gateways to the kingdom of Babylon was decorated with glazed bricks in the form of lions.

ESTHER

Esther, Chapters 1–10

CHAPTER 9 VERSE 21

"... to have them celebrate annually..."

Mordecai orders that the Jews should hold a yearly festival celebrating their escape from Haman's plot. This festival, called Purim, is still celebrated.

Esther was the beautiful Jewish wife of King Xerxes of Persia, who had been raised by her cousin Mordecai. The king had a high official, called Haman, who wanted everybody to bow down to him. When Mordecai refused to do this, Haman planned to take revenge by killing all the Jews in the Persian Empire. He told Xerxes that some people were not obeying the law, and got Xerxes' permission to kill them. Haman then sent out orders to kill the Jews. When Mordecai learned of Haman's plan, he told Esther.

Xerxes

QUEEN OF PERSIA

King Xerxes wanted to find a new queen, so all the young, beautiful women of his empire were brought to the palace for him to choose from. Xerxes chose Esther, whom he loved more than the rest, and had her crowned queen. He did not know that she was Jewish.

Esther is crowned by Xerxes, making her the Queen of Persia.

ESTHER SAVES HER PEOPLE

Upon hearing about Haman's murderous plot from Mordecai, Esther invited Haman and the king to a feast. Here she told Xerxes about Haman's plot to kill all the Jews, which included her. The king was furious and ordered that Haman be executed.

Xerxes gives orders for Haman to be put to death.

Haman is arrested.

Esther

JOB

Job, Chapters 1–2, 38–42

There was a rich man called Job, who lived in the land of Uz. He was a good man who loved and feared God. Job had seven sons and three daughters, and owned many cattle, sheep, and camels. One day, God asked his servant, Satan (Hebrew for "enemy"), if he knew about Job. Satan said that the only reason Job was good was because God had blessed him. He said that if Job lost his children and wealth, he would soon curse God. To see if this was true, God decided to test Job's faith.

GOD SPEAKS TO JOB

God allowed Satan to kill Job's children and animals. Satan even struck Job with painful sores. Job had three friends who told him that his suffering must be punishment for doing wrong. Job knew he had done nothing wrong and asked God to explain. In the end God spoke to him from a storm, and Job realized that he could not understand all God's mysteries. God rewarded Job for his faith.

The **"Satan"** **in this** story is a **servant** of God.

CHAPTER 42 VERSE 3

"... I spoke of things I did not understand..."

Job tells God that he is sorry for having questioned him. God then gives Job double the amount of wealth and children he had had before.

CHAPTER 42 VERSE 7

"I am angry... because you have not spoken the truth about me..."

God is angry with Job's three friends for trying to convince Job that he deserved punishment.

NEHEMIAH

Nehemiah, Chapters 1-2

Nehemiah goes out at night to inspect the walls.

REBUILDING THE WALLS

After reaching Jerusalem, Nehemiah went out at night to inspect the toppled walls and burned gates. The next day, he gave orders to start the rebuilding. It took fifty-two days for the walls to be rebuilt.

Nehemiah was the cupbearer of King Artaxerxes of Persia, serving his drinks at every meal. One day, the king asked Nehemiah why he looked so sad. He replied that it was because the city of Jerusalem, where his people came from, still lay in ruins, after Nebuchadnezzar had captured it. He asked the king for permission to go to Jerusalem to start rebuilding it. King Artaxerxes gladly gave his permission, and sent Nehemiah there with armed horsemen to protect him on his journey.

CHAPTER 2 VERSE 1

"... in the twentieth year of King Artaxerxes..."

King Artaxerxes ruled the Persian Empire from 465-424 BCE. His empire included Jerusalem and Babylon, which the Persians had conquered in 539 BCE.

EZRA

Nehemiah, Chapter 8

CHAPTER 8 VERSE 1

"... Ezra the teacher..."

Ezra was an official, responsible for Jewish affairs. Persian kings respected the different customs and religions of the people they ruled.

Ezra was a priest and a scribe in the service of King Artaxerxes. The king respected Ezra's knowledge of the Jewish religion and thought that Ezra would be a good teacher for the Jews who had returned to Jerusalem. So Ezra travelled to Jerusalem, taking with him a copy of the Torah, the holy book containing the Laws given to Moses. After Nehemiah had rebuilt the walls of Jerusalem, the people all gathered in front of a city gate. They called for Ezra, who climbed onto a high wooden platform, and read to them from the holy book.

A FRESH START

As Ezra read from the Torah, his listeners were overcome with emotion and began to weep. But Ezra told them that this was a holy day, which they should celebrate with joy rather than weeping. It marked a new beginning for the Jewish people, who had safely returned to Jerusalem.

Ezra **read out** the Torah from **daybreak until noon**.

The people bow down and worship God.

THREE WISE MEN
In the New Testament, three wise men, called Magi, travel from the east to Bethlehem to see the baby Jesus. This 6th-century CE mosaic from a church in Ravenna, Italy, shows them bringing gifts for the baby.

2 THE NEW TESTAMENT

The New Testament is the second part of the Christian Bible. It is a collection of books, originally in Greek, written by the followers of Jesus in the latter half of the first century CE. It tells the story of Jesus and the birth of Christianity.

THE NEW TESTAMENT

The New Testament's message is that Jesus Christ was the Messiah, meaning "anointed one" – a holy king, whose coming was foretold by Old Testament prophets. Christ is the Greek word for Messiah. The book begins with four versions of Jesus's life story, called Gospels. These are followed by the Acts of the Apostles, which tells the story of the early Church. There are also twenty-two letters, written by early Christian leaders. Jesus did not leave any writings, but his teachings were recorded by his followers.

MIRACLES AND PARABLES

The New Testament describes many miracles, or seemingly impossible acts, performed by Jesus. The first three Gospels also include many of Jesus's teachings in the form of stories, called parables. This painting depicts the well-known parable of the prodigal son, where a father gladly welcomes back his son, who has wasted his inheritance.

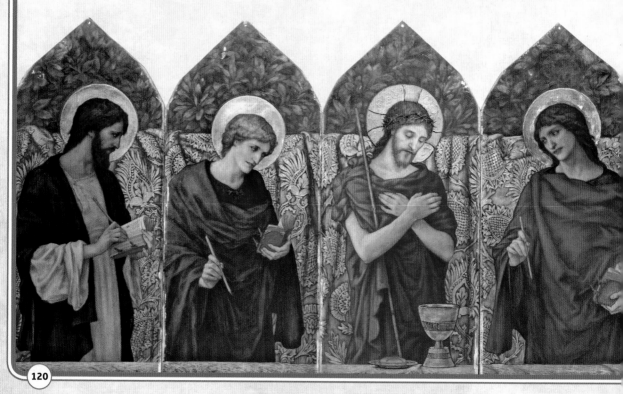

THE BOOK OF REVELATION

This is the last book in the New Testament. It describes a series of visions, including one of Jesus's return, which the author, John, had on the Greek island of Patmos. The above illustration is from a 10th-century Spanish manuscript, showing an angel giving John his message to deliver.

PAUL'S LETTERS

The oldest books in the New Testament are made up of letters written by St Paul between 50–65 CE. Paul travelled widely around the eastern Mediterranean, preaching and founding new Christian communities.

GOSPEL WRITERS

The Gospels (meaning "good news") were written to tell the story of Jesus and present his teachings. The books do not mention the names of their authors, though Church tradition later assigned them to Matthew, Mark, Luke, and John. They are shown here (left), on either side of Jesus.

CHRISTIAN FESTIVALS

Christians mark the major events of Jesus's life with festivals. The most important is Easter, in memory of his death and resurrection (rising from the dead). It begins with Palm Sunday (above) when Christians remember Jesus's final entry into Jerusalem. Palm leaves are waved on Palm Sunday because, according to the Gospels, the crowd carried palm leaves when celebrating Jesus's arrival in the city.

ZECHARIAH

Luke, Chapter 1

CHAPTER 1 VERSE 15

"... he will be filled with the Holy Spirit..."

The angel tells Zechariah that his son John will be a special prophet and that the Holy Spirit will be with him from birth.

Zechariah was a priest, serving in the temple of Jerusalem when Herod was king of Judea (Judah). Zechariah and his wife Elizabeth were both good people who obeyed God's commandments. Yet they were sad because they were old and had no children. One day, Zechariah was performing his duty of burning incense inside the temple, when suddenly the angel Gabriel appeared before him. Zechariah was terrified. Gabriel told Zechariah not to be afraid, and said that his wife would bear a son, who was to be called John. He also said that John would grow up to be a great prophet.

The angel Gabriel appears to Zechariah in the Temple.

STRUCK DUMB

Zechariah told Gabriel that he could not believe that he would have a son. To punish Zechariah for doubting him, the angel took away Zechariah's power of speech. Gabriel said, "You will not be able to speak a single word until what I have told you comes true."

Zechariah

Zechariah looks up in terror.

ELIZABETH

Luke, Chapter 1

As promised by Gabriel, Elizabeth gave birth to a son. Eight days after his birth, the child was to be circumcised and given a name. Elizabeth's family and friends gathered, expecting that the boy would be called Zechariah after his father, as was the custom. But Elizabeth said, "No. He is to be called John." Everyone looked at Zechariah, who had not been able to say a word since his meeting with the angel. He called for a writing tablet, and wrote down, "His name is John." His power of speech returned immediately, and he began to speak, praising God.

ZECHARIAH SPEAKS

When he was able to speak again, Zechariah was filled with the Holy Spirit. He told them all that John would grow up to be a great prophet. Looking down at his baby, Zechariah said, "You will go on before the Lord to prepare the way for him." Everyone was astonished.

When Zechariah writes down the baby's name, he is able to speak again.

The relatives wait to see what the baby will be called.

Elizabeth says the baby's name is John.

MARY

Gabriel

Gabriel tells Mary that God has chosen her to be the mother of his son.

Mary

Mary, the young cousin of Elizabeth's, lived in the town of Nazareth, in Galilee. She was engaged to be married to Joseph, a carpenter. Six months after visiting Zechariah, the angel Gabriel appeared to Mary while she was alone. He greeted her saying, "The Lord is with you." Mary was troubled, and she wondered what the greeting meant. Gabriel told her not to be afraid. He said she would give birth to a son, and she was to call him Jesus. The angel said that her child would be the Son of God, ruling a kingdom that would never end.

SON OF GOD

Mary asked the angel how she could have a child when she was not married. Gabriel answered that nothing was impossible for God, and that the Holy Spirit would make it happen.

CHAPTER 1 VERSE 46

"My soul glorifies the Lord…"

After hearing that she will bear God's son, Mary visits Elizabeth, and both of them rejoice at the news. Mary also sings a beautiful song praising God.

The New Testament

JOSEPH

Matthew, Chapter 1

Joseph was a carpenter who lived in Nazareth, though his family was from Bethlehem, and were descendants of David. Before his wedding to Mary, Joseph found that she was already with child. Thinking the baby's father must be another man, Joseph made up his mind to divorce Mary quietly, without telling anybody that she was pregnant. But an angel appeared to him and told him to keep Mary as his wife, for her baby came from the Holy Spirit.

It was foretold that the **Messiah** would come from **the family of David**.

Angel

The angel tells Joseph to keep Mary as his wife.

JOSEPH'S DREAM

An angel came to Joseph in a dream, and told him not to be afraid to take Mary home as his wife. Joseph did as the angel commanded. By raising Mary's son as his own, Joseph fulfilled a prophecy that the Messiah would be a "Son of David".

Joseph

JESUS IS BORN

Luke, Chapter 2

During his reign, the Roman Emperor, Augustus Caesar, issued a decree that a census should be held of everyone living in the Roman Empire. This meant that people had to go back to their home towns to be registered. So Joseph had to travel from Nazareth to Bethlehem, his birthplace, which lay to the far south. He set off with Mary, who was soon to have her baby. It was in Bethlehem that Mary gave birth to a son, named Jesus. This fulfilled the words of the Prophet Micah, who had said that Bethlehem would be the birthplace of a ruler of Israel.

Bethlehem is about **112 km** (70 miles) south of **Nazareth**.

IN BETHLEHEM

When they arrived in Bethlehem, Joseph and Mary found the place crowded with people who had come there for the census. The people formed long queues, waiting to be registered by the Roman official, who was guarded by soldiers.

Mary and Joseph arrive in Bethlehem.

IN A MANGER

There was no room available in the inns of Bethlehem. Joseph and Mary could only find a shelter in a place where animals were kept. Here, Mary gave birth to her baby boy. She wrapped him in a cloth and laid him in the manger, where the animals usually fed.

ROMAN CENSUS

A census was a register, or list, of people living under Roman rule. It was made so the Romans knew how much tax to charge. The Jewish people hated the census because it was a reminder that they lived under the power of the Romans.

Augustus Caesar

Joseph

The animals witness Jesus's birth.

Mary wraps her baby and places him in the manger.

Mary

THE SHEPHERDS AND THE ANGELS

Luke, Chapter 2

On the night Jesus was born, some shepherds were keeping watch over their flocks in fields near Bethlehem. Suddenly, the dark sky was lit up by an angel, who appeared above them. The shepherds were terrified, but the angel told them not to be afraid. He had brought good news that would bring joy to everybody. That very night, he said, a saviour had been born in Bethlehem, the town where King David was born. The angel told the shepherds to go to Bethlehem, where they would find the baby lying in a manger.

CHOIR OF ANGELS

Suddenly, the first angel was joined by hundreds of others, stretching across the sky. The angels all joined together in a heavenly choir, singing, "Glory to God in the highest heaven, and on earth peace to men on whom his favour rests."

The angel tells the shepherds the news of Jesus's birth.

The shepherds look up in fear.

The sky is filled with angels singing a song of praise.

THE STORY IN ART

The story of the shepherds and angels has often been depicted in art, used to decorate churches, as well as books. This painting from an 11th-century manuscript shows the angel announcing the news of Jesus's birth to the shepherds.

King David was also a **shepherd** from Bethlehem.

The shepherds gaze at baby Jesus.

Joseph and Mary are amazed at the shepherds' story.

TO BETHLEHEM

When the angels left, the shepherds decided to go to Bethlehem to see the newborn baby. Leaving their flocks, they hurried off and found Mary, Joseph, and the baby, who was lying in a manger (a container which held food for animals). They told Mary and Joseph everything they had seen that night. Then they returned to their flocks, praising God.

HEROD THE GREAT

Matthew, Chapter 2

Herod

HEROD QUESTIONS THE PRIESTS

Herod was worried when he heard about the birth of a new king. He asked the priests and teachers of the Law where the baby was likely to be found. They said that according to a prophecy made by the Old Testament prophet Micah, a king would be born in Bethlehem.

Jesus was born at the **end of King Herod the Great's reign**.

When Jesus was born, Judea was ruled by King Herod the Great. At the time, the Romans allowed kings who were loyal to them to rule parts of the Roman Empire. One day, three Magi (wise men) came to visit the king in his palace. The Magi told Herod that they had seen a new star in the sky, and they had followed it all the way from the east to Jerusalem. The Magi believed the star was a sign that a new king had been born, and they had come to worship him.

HEROD AND THE MAGI

Herod advised the Magi to carry on with their search. He asked them to tell him when they found the baby, so that he, too, could worship the new king. However, Herod planned to kill the baby.

The Magi promise to tell Herod where he can find the baby.

Herod fears that the baby would someday threaten his power.

TO BETHLEHEM

The Magi left Herod's palace, and followed the star as it moved across the sky. Eventually it stopped over the place where Mary, Joseph, and Jesus were staying in Bethlehem. Overjoyed, the Magi went inside to see the newborn king.

The star stops over Jesus's birthplace in Bethlehem.

GIFTS FOR JESUS

When they saw the baby, the Magi bowed down before Jesus, offering him gifts of gold, frankincense, and myrrh. They then set off homewards, but did not return to Herod's palace in Jerusalem. They had been warned in a dream not to go back there.

JOHN THE BAPTIST
Luke, Chapter 3

When John, the son of Zechariah and Elizabeth, grew up, he went to live alone in the wilderness. There he heard the word of God and became a prophet. John then went to the countryside on the east side of the River Jordan, where he preached to the people. He told them to repent and turn away from sin. John offered to wash away the people's sins by plunging them in the waters of the River Jordan. Soon word spread, and crowds of people started coming to the river to have their sins washed away by John, who became known as John the Baptist.

CHAPTER 3 VERSE 4
"Prepare the way..."
John says that he is preparing the way for the Messiah. By asking people to turn away from sin, and baptising them, he is making them ready for the coming of Jesus.

✥

CHAPTER 3 VERSE 8
"Produce fruit in keeping with repentance."
Producing fruit here means doing good. John tells his listeners that repentance means changing the way they live their lives.

John wears rough clothes of camel hair.

PREPARING THE WAY
Those who heard John speak wondered if he might be the Messiah they were waiting for. John denied this, but said that the coming of the Messiah was close at hand. He said he had come to prepare the way for the one whose sandals he was not worthy to untie.

The people listening to John wonder if he is the Messiah.

The word **"baptise"** comes from a Greek word meaning **"to plunge"**.

BAPTISM
John plunged his followers beneath the waters of the River Jordan, to baptise them. By doing this, he showed people that they were being washed clean of their sins. But this would only work if the person being baptised sincerely repented.

Tax collectors ask John if they can be baptised.

Roman soldiers listen to John.

BETTER LIVES
John told his followers how they could lead better lives. He said they should share their possessions with those who were poorer. When tax collectors and soldiers came to ask for his advice, he told them not to misuse their power, but to treat people fairly.

AL-MAGHTAS

The ruins at Al-Maghtas, along the River Jordan, are thought to be the place where John baptised people, including Jesus. Many Christian pilgrims still visit this site in Jordan to be baptised.

THE DOVE AND THE DEVIL

Matthew, Chapters 3–4

Jesus travelled south from Galilee to the River Jordan, to be baptised by John the Baptist. Seeing Jesus, John knew that he was not a sinner and had no need to repent. John said, "I need to be baptised by you." But Jesus said that it was God's will that John should baptise him. After this was done, Jesus went into the desert, where he spent forty days in prayer. Here the devil came to Jesus and tempted him with promises of power. The devil asked Jesus to perform miracles to show that he was the Son of God, but Jesus resisted all the devil's temptations.

John the Baptist

Jesus

John baptises Jesus in the River Jordan.

The Holy Spirit appears as a dove.

THE SPIRIT OF GOD

As John lifted Jesus out of the water, the Spirit of God appeared in the form of a dove, hovering over Jesus's head. God then said, "This is my Son, whom I love; with him I am well pleased."

BAPTISM TODAY

Christians around the world are still baptised. Often, this is done by sprinkling drops of water on a baby's head. In some churches, adults are baptised by being plunged into water, just as John baptised Jesus.

Angels appear to help Jesus after his struggle with the devil's temptations.

The devil asks Jesus to show he is the Son of God by throwing himself off the temple roof, while remaining unharmed.

THE TEMPTATIONS OF JESUS

The devil took Jesus to the top of a mountain and showed him the kingdoms of the world. He promised to make Jesus the ruler of them all, if he would only worship the devil instead of God. But Jesus said, "Away from me, Satan!" The devil then left him.

When Jesus is hungry, the devil asks him to turn stones into bread.

In the **Bible** the **devil** is sometimes **called** "**Satan**", which means "**enemy**".

THE DISCIPLES

Mark, Chapters 1–4, 6

In Capernaum, a town by the Sea of Galilee, Jesus gathered his first disciples (pupils), both men and women. From these disciples, Jesus chose an inner group of twelve special followers, called apostles, which means "messengers". Some of them were ordinary fishermen. They included two sets of brothers, Peter (Simon) and Andrew, and James and John. The apostles travelled everywhere with Jesus, learning from his teachings and miracles. Jesus gave them the power to heal the sick and to cast out devils. Privately, Jesus prepared the disciples for his death and taught them how to continue his work.

TWELVE MESSENGERS

Jesus sent the apostles out in pairs to spread his teaching far and wide. He told them to take no food, money, or other belongings with them. As John the Baptist had done, the apostles preached that the Kingdom of Heaven (God's rule over humankind) was arriving, so people needed to repent and turn away from sin.

Philip

Bartholomew (Nathanael)

James

John

Peter (Simon)

Andrew

Matthew (Levi)

Unlike the others, Matthew, also called Levi, is a tax collector.

There were **twelve apostles** just as there were the **Twelve Tribes of Israel.**

THE WOMEN DISCIPLES

Jesus's disciples included women, which was unusual for a religious teacher of the time. According to Luke's gospel, Jesus had cured these women of evil spirits and diseases. They were the first to visit Jesus's tomb after his death, as shown in the painting here.

Jesus

The apostles give up their old lives to follow Jesus.

James, son of Alphaeus

Judas Iscariot will later betray Jesus.

Simon, the Zealot

Thaddaeus (Judas)

Jesus calls the twelve apostles to follow him.

Thomas

Judas Iscariot

SIMON (PETER) AND ANDREW

Luke, Chapter 5

CASTING THE NETS

After lowering their nets as Jesus instructed, so many fish were caught that when the fishermen lifted them, the nets started to break. Simon and Andrew waved at the second fishing boat, which was crewed by James and John (future apostles of Jesus), to come and help them. Soon both the boats were so full of fish that they began to sink. The fishermen had never seen such a big catch.

Jesus went to live in Capernaum, beside the freshwater lake called the Sea of Galilee. On the shore one morning, he saw two fishing boats. One belonged to a fisherman called Simon (later known as Peter), who worked with his brother Andrew. Jesus got into Simon's boat and told the brothers to guide their boat out into deeper waters and to let down the fishing nets. Simon agreed to do this, but said that they had worked hard all night without catching anything. However, when they let down their nets where Jesus told them, they caught so many fish that the nets began to break.

Jesus later gave **Simon** the name **"Peter"**, meaning **"rock"**.

FISHING IN GALILEE

Fishermen still catch fish in the Sea of Galilee, casting nets just as Simon (Peter) and Andrew had done. The main catch is a fish called tilapia, which is known locally as St Peter's fish.

CHAPTER 5 VERSE 10

"... from now on you will fish for people."

Jesus tells the brothers to follow him. He tells them that from now on, instead of catching fish, their work will be to bring people to God.

FOLLOW ME

Back on the shore, Simon and Andrew unloaded their huge catch. Simon knelt before Jesus, and called him Lord. Jesus told the brothers not to be afraid, but to follow him and become his disciples.

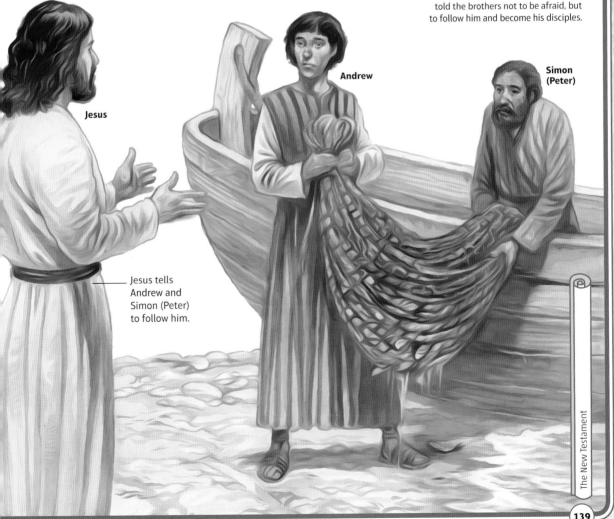

Jesus

Andrew

Simon (Peter)

Jesus tells Andrew and Simon (Peter) to follow him.

JAMES AND JOHN

Mark, Chapters 1, 3; **Luke**, Chapter 9

MARK
CHAPTER 3 VERSE 17

"sons of thunder"

Jesus gives the brothers a nickname, "Boanerges", meaning "sons of thunder". The Gospel does not give a reason for the nickname, but it is likely to have been because of their hot tempers.

THE BROTHERS ANGER JESUS

Jesus and his apostles were once unable to find shelter for the night in a Samaritan village. In anger, James and John asked Jesus if he wanted them to call down fire from heaven to destroy the village. Jesus rebuked them for this, and instead they sought shelter in a different village.

The brothers James and John were fishermen from Galilee. They were the sons of Zebedee, who was also a fisherman. After calling Simon (Peter) to be his follower, Jesus found James and John sitting in their boat, mending fishing nets alongside their father. Jesus called the brothers and at once they left their father to follow him. The brothers were known to be hot tempered, and Jesus had to sometimes scold them for their rashness. James was later beheaded by King Herod Agrippa I, and is the only one of the apostles whose death is recorded in the Bible.

John

James

Jesus rebukes John and James for their hot-headedness.

The brothers call for the destruction of the Samaritan village.

MATTHEW (LEVI)

Mark, Chapter 2

CHAPTER 2 VERSE 16

"Why does he eat with tax collectors...?"

When the Pharisees question Jesus, he tells them that he has not come to call righteous people, but sinners, such as tax collectors.

Matthew, also called Levi, was the fifth person to be chosen by Jesus as his follower. Unlike the others, who were fishermen, Matthew was a tax collector. He worked for Herod Antipas, the ruler of Galilee. After being chosen, Matthew invited Jesus to a big feast at his house. Jesus and his disciples went to the feast and ate with Matthew and his friends, who were also tax collectors. The local Pharisees, teachers of the Law, were shocked to see Jesus eating with tax collectors, who were considered sinners.

JESUS CALLS MATTHEW

Jesus first saw Matthew while walking by the Sea of Galilee. Matthew was sitting at his booth, collecting taxes from the people. Jesus went up to him and said, "Follow me". Matthew, astonished to be chosen, got up at once and became Jesus's follower.

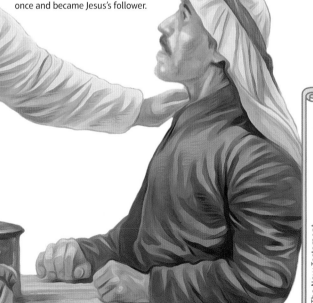

Jesus calls Matthew to follow him.

THE TRANSFIGURATION

Matthew, Chapters 16-17

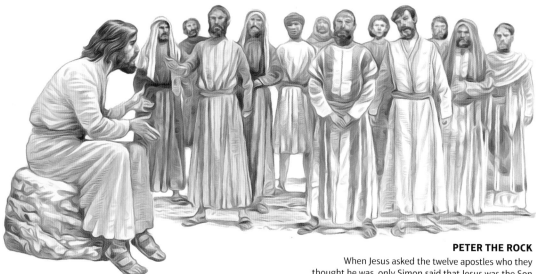

PETER THE ROCK

When Jesus asked the twelve apostles who they thought he was, only Simon said that Jesus was the Son of God. Jesus was so pleased with him that he gave him the name "Peter", meaning "rock". Jesus said that Peter was like a rock, on which he would build his church.

In Caesarea Philippi, Jesus asked his apostles who the people thought he was. They replied that people said he was a prophet from the past, such as Elijah, who had been reborn. Jesus then asked the apostles who they thought he was. Only Simon replied that Jesus was "the Messiah, the Son of the living God". Jesus then told the apostles that he had to go to Jerusalem, where he would suffer and die at the hands of the priests, but that he would rise again on the third day after his death. The apostles were shocked to hear this, but Jesus told them that it was God's will.

Peter does not want Jesus to suffer.

GOD'S WILL

When Peter heard that Jesus had to suffer and die, he said "Never, Lord! This shall never happen to you!" Jesus told Peter that he was only thinking of himself and not the will of God.

Moses

Jesus

Elijah

THE TRANSFIGURATION

Six days later, Jesus took Peter and the brothers James and John up to a high mountain. Here, Jesus was transfigured and shone like a heavenly being, while Moses and Elijah appeared beside him. A bright cloud covered Jesus, and a voice from the cloud said, "This is my Son, whom I love." The disciples were terrified and fell to the ground, with their face down. But Jesus came to them and told them to not be afraid. When the disciples looked up, they saw only Jesus, no longer shining.

The New Testament

THE SERMON ON THE MOUNT

Matthew, Chapters 5–7

As news of Jesus's teachings and healing ability spread, great crowds came to listen to him. One day, so that he could be heard better, Jesus went up on the side of a mountain with his disciples. There he sat down and spoke to the crowd gathered below. Jesus said that the meek, the merciful, the pure in heart, and the peacemakers would all be blessed. He told the people that even though they suffered on earth, they would be rewarded in heaven. He then talked about the Law of Moses, and said that he had not come to change them but to fulfil them.

The twelve apostles sit closest to Jesus.

Jesus speaks to the crowd from the mountainside.

LOVE YOUR ENEMIES

In his sermon, Jesus told the people not to resist an evil person. He said if someone struck them on one cheek, they should offer the other cheek to be struck as well. Even though some people had said, love your neighbour and hate your enemy, Jesus said, "I tell you to love your enemies".

CHAPTER 5 VERSE 3

"Blessed are the..."

The opening words in Jesus's speech are known as the "Beatitudes", which is Latin for "blessed" or "fortunate". Jesus lists eight groups of people who would be blessed by God, or rewarded after death in heaven.

SITE OF THE SERMON

This church, called the Church of the Beatitudes, stands on a hill by the Sea of Galilee. It is thought to be the place where Jesus gave his sermon. The church has eight sides, one for each of the eight groups that Jesus said would be blessed.

The New Testament

MIRACLES

Mark, Chapters 4–5; **Matthew**, Chapter 14; **John**, Chapter 2

Jesus astonished people by his ability to work miracles, acts which no ordinary human could perform. The Gospels tell how he healed the sick, raised the dead, calmed storms, turned water into wine, walked on water, and fed five thousand people with only five loaves of bread and two fishes. Jesus worked miracles to show his disciples and the people that anything was possible if only they believed in him.

Jesus

FEEDING THE FIVE THOUSAND

After teaching a crowd of five thousand people, Jesus told his disciples to give the people something to eat. The disciples said that they had only five loaves of bread and two fishes. Jesus took this food and broke it into pieces. The disciples handed out the pieces and miraculously there was enough food for everyone to eat.

The disciples are amazed to see Jesus create more food for the people.

CALMING THE STORM

Jesus and the disciples were once crossing the Sea of Galilee when a terrible storm broke out. The frightened disciples woke Jesus, who had been sleeping. Jesus stood up, and said to the waves, "Quiet! Be still!" At once, the sea grew calm.

THE FIRST MIRACLE

Jesus's first miracle was at a wedding feast at Cana, in Galilee. When the wine at the feast ran out, Jesus told the servants to fill six large jars with water, and then serve this to the guests. When they poured the water into cups, it had turned to wine.

"Miracle" is taken from the **Latin word *miraculum*,** meaning **"object of wonder"**.

WALKING ON WATER

One night, Jesus asked his apostles to get into a boat and cross the Sea of Galilee while he stayed back to pray. Just before dawn, the boat was quite a distance from land. Then suddenly, the apostles in the boat saw Jesus walking towards them across the water. Peter got out of the boat and started to walk towards Jesus, but grew afraid and immediately began to sink. Jesus grasped his hands and pulled him out, asking, "why did you doubt?"

Jesus grasps Peter's hands and saves him from drowning.

Peter

The New Testament

PARABLES

Luke, Chapter 10; **Matthew**, Chapter 18; **Mark**, Chapter 4

THE PRIEST AND THE LEVITE
Jesus told the story of a Jewish man travelling from Jerusalem, who was attacked and left for dead by robbers. First a priest and then a Levite (a man who helped the priests in the temple) passed by. Both of them walked past on the other side of the road without helping him.

The priest sees the man but does not stop.

Levite

Jesus taught people by telling stories drawn from everyday life. These were called parables. The word "parable" is Greek and means placing two things side by side, to compare them. In one parable, for example, Jesus compared the Kingdom of God to a mustard plant (see right). He also often told parables as a way of answering questions. One day, an expert in the Law asked Jesus what he had to do to be saved. Jesus told him to love God and his neighbour. The man then asked, "who is my neighbour?" To answer the question, Jesus told him a parable about a good Samaritan (someone from Samaria).

The Samaritan tends to the traveller's wounds.

THE SAMARITAN SHOWS MERCY

Then a Samaritan arrived. Although Samaritans and Jews usually hated each other, he took pity on the injured man, bandaging his wounds and looking after him. Jesus asked who in the story was the neighbour of the man. The answer was the one who had mercy on the traveller.

Several of **Jesus's parables describe** the **Kingdom of God**.

Oil

Linen bandages

Wine

THE LOST SHEEP

Jesus also told the parable of a shepherd who lost a single sheep from a flock of a hundred. When he finally found the stray sheep, he was overjoyed. In fact, the shepherd was happier about finding the lost sheep than about the ninety-nine that did not wander off. The lost sheep represents a sinner who is saved by Jesus, the good shepherd.

The lost sheep is found.

MUSTARD PLANT

Black mustard stalk

In another parable, Jesus told his listeners to think about the mustard plant. It has the tiniest seed, yet it grows into one of the tallest garden plants. In the same way, great things, such as the Kingdom of God, can grow from small beginnings.

HEROD ANTIPAS AND SALOME

Matthew, Chapter 14

Herod Antipas, son of Herod the Great, was the ruler of Galilee. Herod had arrested John, and locked him up in prison. This was because John had criticized Herod for marrying his brother's wife, Herodias. John said that what Herod had done was against God's laws. Herodias disliked John for saying this about her marriage. She wanted Herod to put John to death. Yet Herod was afraid to kill John, for the people of Galilee believed that John was a prophet. Later, when Herod heard reports of Jesus's teaching and miracles, he wondered if Jesus was John the Baptist come back to life.

SALOME'S DANCE

Herodias' daughter was called Salome. At Herod's birthday celebrations, Salome danced for him. Her dance pleased him so much that he swore to give her anything she desired. Prompted by her mother, she asked him for the head of John the Baptist. Herod was horrified, but he could not refuse her because he had sworn an oath.

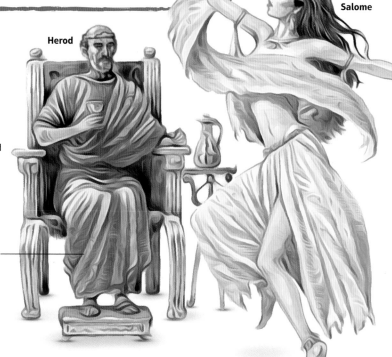

Herod

Salome

Herod watches with delight as Salome dances.

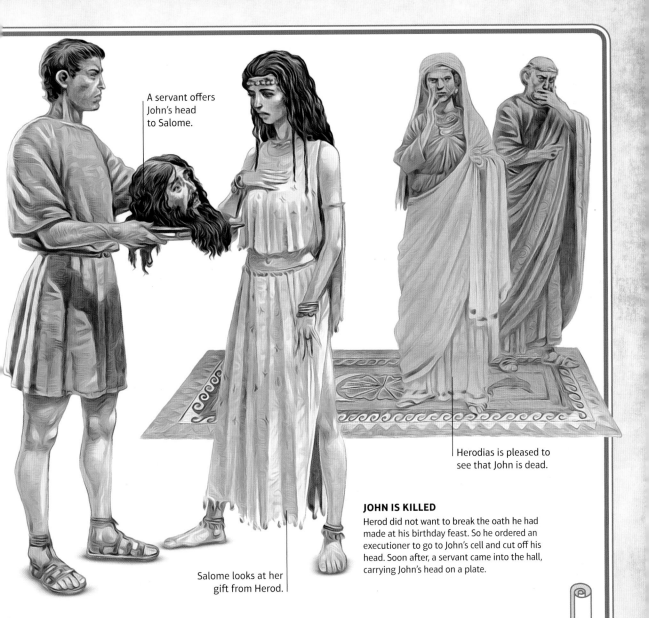

A servant offers John's head to Salome.

Herodias is pleased to see that John is dead.

Salome looks at her gift from Herod.

JOHN IS KILLED

Herod did not want to break the oath he had made at his birthday feast. So he ordered an executioner to go to John's cell and cut off his head. Soon after, a servant came into the hall, carrying John's head on a plate.

The name **"Salome"** is from the **Hebrew word** *shalom* meaning **"peace"**.

HEROD THE TETRARCH

Herod Antipas governed a small part of his father's kingdom, including Galilee. His title was not "king" but "tetrarch", which means "governor of a quarter". He ruled from 4 BCE to 39 CE.

Coins from the reign of Herod Antipas

The New Testament

ZACCHAEUS

Luke, Chapter 19

Zacchaeus was a rich tax collector who lived in the city of Jericho. On his way to Jerusalem, Jesus passed through Jericho. The people, who had heard stories of his teachings and miracles, came out to the streets to see him. Zacchaeus was among them, but he was a short man and could not see Jesus because of the crowd. So he climbed a sycamore tree to get a proper look. As Jesus passed by, he looked up at the tree and said, "Zacchaeus, come down immediately. I must stay at your house today." Zacchaeus came down from the tree and gladly welcomed Jesus.

Zacchaeus sits in a sycamore tree.

The people are angry that Jesus talks to a tax collector.

VISITING ZACCHAEUS

At this time, tax collectors such as Zacchaeus were unpopular. The crowd complained that Jesus had gone to visit a sinner. But Zacchaeus was deeply moved that Jesus had chosen to stay with him. He promised to give half his possessions to the poor, and said that if he had cheated anybody, he would repay them four times the amount he had taken.

TAX COLLECTORS

Although many tax collectors at the time were Jews, they were looked down on by other Jews as sinners. This was because they worked for the despised Romans, and often made themselves rich by overcharging people. This Roman carving shows a tax collector keeping records.

CHAPTER 19 VERSE 9

"... this man, too, is a son of Abraham."

Tax collectors were not seen as true Jews (sons of Abraham). But Jesus welcomes Zacchaeus back into Jewish society.

✛

CHAPTER 19 VERSE 10

"For the Son of Man came to seek and to save the lost."

Jesus says he has come to save people who have lost their way in life. By repenting for his sins, Zacchaeus, the tax collector, has been saved.

Jesus calls up to Zacchaeus.

The people of Jericho come out to see Jesus.

LAZARUS

John, Chapter 11

"Jesus wept" is one of the **shortest verses** in the English Bible.

Lazarus lived in Bethany, near Jerusalem, with his sisters Martha and Mary, who were followers of Jesus. One day, the sisters sent Jesus a message that Lazarus was gravely ill. When Jesus reached Bethany, he met Martha, who told him that her brother was already dead, and had been buried for four days. "If only you had been here", she said, "my brother would not have died." Jesus told her that her brother would live again, saying "He who believes in me will live, even though he dies." Jesus then went to the tomb to raise Lazarus from the dead.

CHAPTER 11 VERSE 25

"I am the resurrection and the life."

Resurrection means "raising up" after death. Jesus says that he offers his followers the chance to live again after death.

CHAPTER 11 VERSE 35

"Jesus wept."

When Jesus sees the mourners weeping, he also weeps, sharing their suffering. This shows that he is human, as well as divine.

Jesus

RISEN FROM THE DEAD

Jesus had the stone blocking Lazarus's tomb rolled away. He looked up and gave thanks out loud to God, his Father, for helping him raise Lazarus. In a loud voice, he then cried, "Lazarus, come out!" To everyone's astonishment, Lazarus walked out of his tomb alive.

Lazarus, his body still wrapped in linen burial clothes, walks out of his dark tomb into the bright daylight.

The people watch in amazement.

TOMB OF LAZARUS

Bethany (modern-day al-Eizariya, Palestine) lies 2.4 km (1.5 miles) east of Jerusalem. This tomb in Bethany dates from the time of Jesus. Since at least the 4th century CE, it has been identified as the tomb of Lazarus. It is a popular site for Christian pilgrims, who wish to retrace Jesus's journey.

The stone has been rolled away.

Lazarus

JESUS ENTERS JERUSALEM

Matthew, Chapter 21

In the week before the Passover festival, Jesus and his followers made their way to Jerusalem. On the way, Jesus sent two disciples into a village, telling them that they would find a donkey and her colt there, which they should fetch. The disciples brought the animals and spread their cloaks on them, and Jesus rode the donkey into the city. Jesus did this to fulfil the words of the prophet Zechariah, who had said, "See, your king comes to you, gentle and riding on a donkey."

HOSANNA!

As they travelled, Jesus and his disciples were joined by many pilgrims, all going to celebrate Passover. Word spread that the Messiah, a new King David, was on his way to Jerusalem. The people spread palm leaves in his path and shouted, "Hosanna to the son of David!" The word "hosanna" means "save us".

THE MONEY CHANGERS IN THE TEMPLE

Mark, Chapter 11

The birds and animals escape from their cages.

Arriving in Jerusalem, Jesus went to the temple, where crowds were getting ready for the festival. In the temple courtyard, he found traders selling cattle, sheep, and doves, to be offered as sacrifices. There were also money changers, who exchanged the people's money into the special coinage used in the temple and made huge profits by cheating pilgrims. Jesus was furious at the sight. He said that the temple was meant to be a place of prayer, but these people had turned it into "a den of robbers".

CLEARING THE COURTYARD

In a fury, Jesus ran around the temple courtyard and tipped over all the traders' tables. He drove all the traders, and their animals, out of the temple courtyard. This angered the corrupt temple priests.

THE LAST SUPPER

Luke, Chapter 22; **Mark**, Chapter 14; **John**, Chapter 13; **Matthew**, Chapter 26

On the eve of the Passover festival, Jesus and his apostles met for a meal in a house in Jerusalem. Jesus broke bread and shared it with the apostles, telling them it was his body. He also offered them his cup of wine, and said it was his blood. Jesus said his death would save people from their sins. He told the apostles that one of them would soon betray him. Each of the apostles said they would never betray him. Peter told Jesus he was willing to go to prison and die with him, but Jesus said that Peter would deny knowing him three times.

JESUS AND JUDAS

Jesus knew that Judas Iscariot planned to betray him. So when he handed Judas a piece of bread, he said, "What you are about to do, do quickly." None of the other apostles knew what Jesus meant, but Judas left the room, and hurried into the night.

Simon
the Zealot

James

Matthew
(Levi)

Thaddaeus
(Judas)

Bartholomew
(Nathanael)

Philip

Andrew

THE UPPER ROOM

This room in Jerusalem called "the cenacle" is thought to have been built on the site of the room used for the Last Supper. It is located near Dormition Abbey, a great church built by Christians more than a thousand years after Jesus's death.

The receiving of the **body and blood** of Jesus is called **"Holy Communion"** today.

Jesus hands Judas a piece of bread.

John

Jesus

Peter

James, son of Alphaeus

Thomas

Judas Iscariot

JUDAS ISCARIOT
Matthew, Chapters 26-27

Judas Iscariot had promised to betray Jesus to the priests. After leaving Jesus and the other apostles at the Last Supper, Judas went to Caiaphas, the High Priest, and told him that he would lead the priests' men to Jesus in exchange for money. Meanwhile, Jesus and the other apostles walked to Gethsemane, an olive grove outside Jerusalem. Jesus knew that he would soon face death, and was deeply troubled. After asking Peter, James, and John to keep watch, Jesus went to one side to pray.

The apostles fall asleep.

Jesus asks God to spare him.

JESUS PRAYS

Jesus asked God if he could be spared from the suffering that lay ahead. He said that he would do whatever God willed. Jesus then went back to the apostles, who had fallen asleep.

A **kiss** was a sign of **affection and respect** between **friends and teachers**.

A KISS OF BETRAYAL

When Jesus was waking up the apostles, he heard Judas approaching. Judas, followed by the temple guards and a large crowd, went to Jesus and kissed him on the cheek. This was a sign, showing the guards that this was the man to arrest. They seized Jesus and took him away.

SILVER COINS

The priests paid Judas thirty silver coins, called shekels, to betray Jesus. He later returned the money, but the priests refused to put it in the temple treasury as it was "blood money". It was used to buy a piece of land that later became a cemetery.

Judas betrays Jesus with a kiss.

CHAPTER 26 VERSE 4

"... they schemed to arrest Jesus secretly and kill him."

By arresting Jesus at night, when few people are around, the priests avoid the risk of a riot breaking out.

✛

CHAPTER 26 VERSE 39

"... may this cup be taken from me."

The cup refers to the suffering Jesus is about to face. He asks God to spare him this, if possible, but promises that he will do whatever his father wishes.

The priests

Judas Iscariot

Jesus knows that Judas has come to betray him.

JUDAS REPENTS

Judas later regretted betraying Jesus, and went to the temple to hand back the money. He said, "I have betrayed innocent blood." He threw the coins at the priests' feet, and later hanged himself.

Judas

JESUS IS TRIED, PETER DENIES

Mark, Chapter 14

SON OF GOD

At first, Jesus refused to answer the priests' questions. Then the High Priest asked him if he was the Messiah, the Son of God. Jesus replied, "I am", and said that they would see him sitting at the right hand of God. To the High Priest, this was blasphemy, an insult to God.

Jesus

After his arrest, Jesus was taken to be questioned by the High Priest and the chief priests. They wanted to find evidence against Jesus, so that they could convince the Romans to put him to death. False witnesses came forward, telling lies about Jesus, which he refused to answer. Meanwhile, Peter, who was waiting outside in the courtyard, was accused of being a follower of Jesus. He denied knowing Jesus three times. This was just as Jesus had foretold at the Last Supper, when he said that Peter would disown him that very night, three times before the cock crowed.

The High Priest tears his clothes when he hears Jesus's reply.

In Roman times, **cock-crowing** was a way of **telling the time**.

SANHEDRIN

This mosaic, from a church in Italy, shows Jesus in front of the Sanhedrin, the chief court of Israel. The Romans used the Sanhedrin to help them keep order in Jerusalem, but they did not allow the court to sentence people to death. The priests needed to find evidence against Jesus to show the Romans that he was guilty.

A servant girl recognizes Peter.

Peter

PETER'S DENIAL
In the courtyard, a servant girl recognized Peter as a follower of Jesus and said, "This fellow is one of them." Peter said he did not know what she was talking about, and that he did not even know who Jesus was.

PONTIUS PILATE

Matthew, Chapter 27

Pontius Pilate, Roman governor of Judea, had come to Jerusalem for the Passover festival, bringing soldiers with him to keep order. The morning after they arrested Jesus, the priests took him to Pilate. They accused Jesus of calling himself king of the Jews, and demanded his death. Jesus refused to answer their charges. Pilate said that he could see no reason to kill Jesus. But the crowd, who had been persuaded by the priests, called for Jesus's death. To please them, Pilate gave orders for Jesus to be crucified (put to death on a cross).

CHAPTER 27 VERSE 24

"... he took water and washed his hands... "

Pilate washes his hands to show that he is not guilty of Jesus's death. Washing hands was a Jewish, not a Roman, way of showing guiltlessness.

Jesus does not answer his accusers.

Pontius Pilate was the **Governor of Judea** for **around ten years**.

The crowd calls for Jesus to be crucified.

JESUS OR BARABBAS?

Each year, at the Passover festival, Pilate would free one prisoner chosen by the crowd. Pilate asked the crowd if he should free Jesus or a murderer called Barabbas. The people shouted "Barabbas". When Pilate asked them what he should do with Jesus, they cried, "Crucify him!"

A crown of thorns is made for Jesus.

The soldiers mock Jesus.

Pontius Pilate

A boy brings a jar of water so Pilate can wash his hands.

THE SOLDIERS MOCK JESUS

The Roman soldiers took Jesus into Pilate's headquarters. They mocked him by making him wear a crown made of thorns and a scarlet robe, like those worn by kings. The soldiers bowed before him mockingly and cried, "Hail, king of the Jews!" They took off the robe before taking Jesus to be crucified.

PILATE'S PALACE

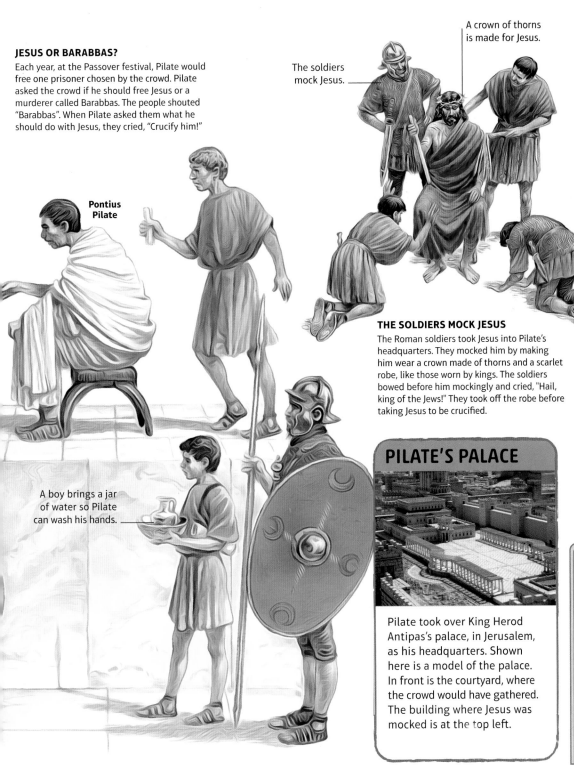

Pilate took over King Herod Antipas's palace, in Jerusalem, as his headquarters. Shown here is a model of the palace. In front is the courtyard, where the crowd would have gathered. The building where Jesus was mocked is at the top left.

JESUS IS CRUCIFIED

Mark, Chapter 15

The Roman soldiers took Jesus out of the city of Jerusalem to be crucified (put to death on a wooden cross). They made him carry the cross on his shoulders. Jesus stumbled under the heavy weight of the cross, so the soldiers forced a bystander to carry it for him. At nine o'clock in the morning, they reached a place called Golgotha, where the soldiers nailed Jesus to the cross. They set the cross upright, and placed a sign above it that mocked Jesus, calling him "The King of the Jews". At the foot of the cross, Jesus's disciples, including Mary Magdalene, watched helplessly as Jesus suffered and died.

"Golgotha" is an **Aramaic** word, meaning **"the place of a skull"**.

Two thieves are crucified with Jesus, one on either side of him.

A Roman soldier stands guard.

ON THE CROSS
At midday, after Jesus had been on the cross for three hours, the sky suddenly grew dark. It stayed dark until three o'clock in the afternoon when, with a loud cry, Jesus breathed his last. Moved by his death, a Roman centurion said, "Surely this man was the Son of God!"

Mary Magdalene and the other women weep for Jesus.

A sign saying "The King of the Jews" is placed at the top of the cross.

Jesus

The centurion comes to believe Jesus is the Son of God.

VIA DOLOROSA

Jesus is thought to have walked along this street in Jerusalem, called the Via Dolorosa, or "way of sorrow". It has fourteen stations – places marking important moments on Jesus's journey. Shown here is the ninth station, where according to tradition Jesus fell for the third time under the weight of the cross.

The priests mock Jesus for not being able to save himself.

JESUS IS MOCKED

The priests mocked Jesus, asking why he did not come down from the cross and save himself if he really was the Son of God. Meanwhile, Roman soldiers cast lots to see which of them could keep Jesus's clothes.

JOSEPH OF ARIMATHEA

John, Chapter 19

A rich Jewish man from Arimathea, Joseph was a secret disciple of Jesus. On the evening of Jesus's crucifixion, Joseph went to Pilate, the Roman governor, and asked him for permission to bury Jesus. Pilate, who did not know that Joseph was a follower of Jesus, gave him permission to take the body. Together with his friend Nicodemus, Joseph went to Golgotha and collected Jesus's body, which they wrapped in strips of linen. Nicodemus had bought expensive spices, myrrh, and aloes, which they placed inside the wrappings. Then they carried Jesus to a tomb, in a nearby garden.

CHAPTER 19 VERSE 38

"... Joseph was a disciple of Jesus, but secretly..."

Fearing the Jewish priests, Joseph keeps it secret that he is a disciple of Jesus. If Pilate knew Joseph was a disciple, he might have refused his request to bury Jesus.

Nicodemus helps Joseph carry Jesus's body.

THE TOMB IN THE GARDEN

Near the place where Jesus was crucified, there was a garden with a tomb, newly cut in the rock. Joseph and Nicodemus carried Jesus's body into the tomb, and laid it down there. Then they rolled a stone in front of the entrance.

Joseph of Arimathea

NICODEMUS
John, Chapter 3

CHAPTER 3 VERSE 1
"Now there was a Pharisee..."
The name "Pharisee" is taken from the Aramaic word for "separate". The Pharisees wanted to separate themselves from anything unholy.

Nicodemus was a member of the Jewish ruling council in Jerusalem. He was a Pharisee, one of the religious teachers who believed that Jewish Law should be strictly followed. Nicodemus had been amazed by Jesus's miracles. To learn more about him, he went to see Jesus at night, in secret, so that his fellow Pharisees did not know about his visit. Nicodemus said that he believed Jesus must be a teacher sent by God, because no one could perform such astonishing miracles unless God was with them.

JESUS TEACHES NICODEMUS

Jesus then said to Nicodemus, "no one can see the kingdom of God unless they are born again." Nicodemus did not understand Jesus and asked, "How can someone be born when they are old?" Jesus replied that he was not talking about a person's body being reborn, but their spirit.

Nicodemus

Jesus

JESUS IS RISEN

Matthew, Chapters 27–28

At dawn on Monday, three days after Jesus's death, Mary Magdalene and Mary, mother of James and Joseph, visited Jesus's tomb. Its entrance was sealed with a big stone, and Pilate had ordered soldiers to guard it. This was because the priests had warned Pilate that Jesus's disciples might steal the body, to make it look like Jesus had risen from the dead. When the women reached the tomb, a great earthquake shook the ground. Then an angel appeared, rolled back the stone, and sat on it. The guards were so scared at the sight of the angel that they fainted.

Jesus rising from the dead is called the **"Resurrection"** in Christianity.

The angel tells the women that Jesus has risen.

THE ANGEL SPEAKS

The angel told the women not to be afraid. He showed them the empty tomb, and said that Jesus had risen from the dead. The angel then asked them to bring the good news to the disciples, and to tell them that they would see Jesus again in Galilee.

JESUS APPEARS

The women hurried away from the tomb, full of joy and fear. Suddenly they saw Jesus standing in front of them. They fell to their knees and worshipped him. Jesus told them not to be afraid, but to tell the apostles what they had seen.

Jesus

Mary

Mary Magdalene

The risen Jesus appears to the women.

BURIAL SITE

Two places in Jerusalem are thought to be the site of Jesus's tomb. One of them has the Church of the Holy Sepulchre (tomb) built over it. The other is the Garden Tomb (shown here), discovered in 1867, which matches the description of the tomb in the Bible.

BRIBING THE GUARDS

The tomb guards told the priests what had happened. The priests gave them a large sum of money, and told them to tell everybody that Jesus's body had been stolen by his disciples.

The priests bribe the guards.

MARY MAGDALENE

Luke, Chapter 8

Mary Magdalene was the most important of Jesus's women disciples. She became his devoted follower after he cast out seven demons that had possessed her. Mary followed Jesus from Galilee to Jerusalem, where she saw him die on the cross. Later, she went to Jesus's tomb to anoint his body with oil and was one of the first people to see him after he rose from the dead.

Jesus talks with Mary Magdalene.

WOMEN FOLLOWERS

Jesus travelled to many towns with his disciples, to spread his message. Mary was one of several women who travelled with him. These women supported Jesus and the apostles using their own means. Another well-known woman disciple was Joanna, whose husband Chuza managed the household of Herod Antipas.

Mary Magdalene

CHAPTER 8 VERSE 2

"... from whom seven demons had come out..."

At this time, many illnesses were thought to be caused by the body being taken over by devils or demons.

CHAPTER 8 VERSE 3

"... out of their own means."

This phrase suggests that Mary, and some of the other women disciples had money, with which they supported Jesus and his apostles. However, we do not know where Mary's money came from.

Mary Magdalene is **named in all four Gospels** in the New Testament.

MAGDALA

Mary's surname suggests that she came from Magdala, an ancient town on the shore of the Sea of Galilee. Archaeologists have found remains of the oldest synagogue in Galilee at the site of Magdala. It is likely that Jesus taught in this very synagogue.

Joanna supported Jesus and the apostles in their travels.

The apostles travel with Jesus.

THOMAS

John, Chapter 20

Thomas, also called Didymus, was one of Jesus's twelve apostles. In the evening, soon after Jesus was resurrected, the apostles met in a house, but Thomas was not with them. Although the door to the house was locked, Jesus suddenly appeared among them. The apostles were overjoyed to see Jesus, who showed them the wounds on his hands and side. Later when they told Thomas that they had seen Jesus, he said he would not believe this unless he saw Jesus with his own eyes and touched the wounds for himself. A week later, the apostles met in the same house, and this time Thomas was with them to see for himself.

THOMAS TOUCHES JESUS
Jesus appeared to the apostles for a second time. He then told Thomas, "Reach out your hand and put it into my side. Stop doubting and believe." Thomas did just this, and realized that it really was Jesus. He cried out, "My Lord and my God!"

CHAPTER 20 VERSE 19

"... with the doors locked..."
Jesus enters the house miraculously, through a locked door. Yet he is not a ghost. According to the Gospel of Luke, he even eats food with the apostles.

✜

CHAPTER 20 VERSE 29

"... blessed are those who have not seen..."
Jesus says that Thomas only believes because he has seen proof. But those who believe without proof are blessed, for their faith is stronger.

Someone who **does not believe without proof** is known as a **"doubting Thomas"**.

THOMAS IN INDIA

According to some stories, Thomas later sailed to India to spread Christianity. This church, at Kodungallur in Kerala, was built to mark the place where he is thought to have landed. It is known as the birthplace of Christianity in India.

Nail wound in Jesus's wrist.

Jesus

Thomas touches the wound where a soldier had pierced Jesus with a spear to make sure he was dead.

THE ASCENSION

Matthew, Chapter 28; **Acts**, Chapter 1

After rising from the dead, Jesus asked the apostles to meet him on a mountain in Galilee. Here Jesus told them to go out and preach to all nations, in the name of the Father, the Son, and the Holy Spirit. He said that although he would shortly leave the apostles, he would always be with them, until the end of time. He then told them to go to Jerusalem, to wait there to receive the gift of the Holy Spirit from his Father. Jesus said, "you will receive power when the Holy Spirit comes on you."

Jesus rises up into the sky. _____

TAKEN UP

After Jesus finished speaking, he was taken up into the sky in front of the apostles' eyes, and a cloud wrapped around him, hiding him from their view. Then two angels appeared on the ground beside the apostles and said that Jesus would one day return to earth just as he had left it.

Two angels appear next to the apostles.

PENTECOST

Acts, Chapters 1-2

CHAPTER 2 VERSE 3

"... tongues of fire..."

The tongues of fire are a visible sign of the presence of the Holy Spirit that the apostles receive. In the Bible, fire is sometimes the way God shows his presence – such as the burning bush Moses encounters in the Old Testament.

The harvest festival of Pentecost followed soon after Jesus's ascension into heaven. Jerusalem was filled with people from many lands, who spoke many languages, visiting for the festival. The apostles met in a house in Jerusalem. Suddenly they heard the noise of a violent wind rushing through the house. Looking at each other, they saw what looked like tongues of fire resting on their heads. They had been filled with the Holy Spirit, just as Jesus had promised. The apostles then went outside to preach to the crowds in Jerusalem.

SPEAKING IN TONGUES

After being filled with the Holy Spirit, when the apostles turned to speak to each other, they were astonished to find themselves talking in different languages. Yet they could all understand every word said. The Holy Spirit had given them this power. Later, when they preached to the crowds in Jerusalem, the people were amazed, because each heard them speaking in their own language.

Tongues of fire

STEPHEN
Acts, Chapters 6–8

Stephen was one of seven men, chosen by the apostles to serve the early Christian community in Jerusalem. Like Jesus, he was put on trial by the Sanhedrin, the court of chief priests. The priests accused him of speaking against the Law of Moses. Stephen said that it was the members of the Sanhedrin who were guilty, for they had murdered the Messiah. The priests were so angry with Stephen's reply that they dragged him out of the city, and stoned him to death.

CHAPTER 7 VERSE 51
"You always resist the Holy Spirit!"
Stephen accuses the Sanhedrin, although he risks death. Someone who willingly accepts death for religious reasons is called a "martyr", from the Greek word for "witness".

✛

CHAPTER 7 VERSE 60
"Lord, do not hold this sin against them."
According to Luke's Gospel, Jesus prayed for forgiveness for those who crucified him. Like Jesus, Stephen's last words here forgive those who kill him.

The apostles bless each of the seven men.

Procorus

Timon

Stephen

Philip

Nicanor

Parmenas

Nicolas

Stephen kneels to be blessed.

SEVEN DEACONS
Stephen was among the seven men who were chosen to serve Jerusalem's Christian community. Their role was to share out food every day to poorer Christians. The apostles chose these men because of their wisdom and holiness. On being chosen, each man was blessed by the apostles. The seven were later called "deacons"– which comes from the Greek word for "servant".

ST STEPHEN'S GATE

Stephen was stoned to death outside this gate in Jerusalem, near the hall in where the Sanhedrin met. It is called St Stephen's Gate by Christians, and the Lions' Gate by everyone else. It is decorated with carved leopards, which were mistaken for lions.

Stephen was the **first Christian martyr**.

Stephen looks up and sees Jesus.

STEPHEN SEES JESUS

After Stephen spoke in front of the Sanhedrin, he gazed upwards. He told the priests that he could see heaven opening, and Jesus standing at the right hand of God. The priests were so angry at Stephen's words that they covered their ears, and later dragged him out of the city to put him to death.

The High Priest is furious at Stephen's words.

PHILIP THE EVANGELIST

Acts, Chapter 8

Saul has many Christians arrested.

HUNTING FOR CHRISTIANS

In Jerusalem, the priests did everything they could to destroy the new Church. Leading the attack was a young man called Saul. He went from house to house, searching for followers of Jesus. Saul had them dragged out and taken away to prison.

Simon envies Philip's power to heal.

Samaritans who see Philip healing become believers.

Philip

After Stephen's death, it was no longer safe for the followers of Jesus to stay in Jerusalem. They scattered in different directions, preaching their faith as they travelled. Philip, Stephen's fellow deacon, travelled north to Samaria. Here he performed many miracles, including healing the sick. Samaritans (people from Samaria) who saw Philip's miracles were so impressed that they, too, became followers of Jesus. From Samaria, Philip travelled along the coast, south to Gaza, and north again to Caesarea. Everywhere he went, Philip preached. He came to be called Philip the Evangelist, meaning "the bearer of good news".

SIMON THE SORCERER

Philip's miracles amazed a Samaritan called Simon, who was a sorcerer. Simon became a Christian, and followed Philip wherever he went. His real aim was to gain Philip's ability to work miracles. Later he offered money to the apostle Peter for this power, but Peter refused.

THE ETHIOPIAN

While travelling south to Gaza, Philip met a high official of the Queen of Ethiopia, in Africa. The official had been to Jerusalem to worship in the temple. Philip found the Ethiopian sitting in his chariot, reading the Book of Isaiah.

Philip offers to explain the Book of Isaiah to the Ethiopian.

CAESAREA

Philip settled in Caesarea, a port city built by King Herod the Great in 22–10 BCE. The city was named in honour of Augustus Caesar. It was a thriving port where most people were Gentiles and a safe base for Christians to preach and spread their message.

CHAPTER 8 VERSE 32

"He was led like a sheep to the slaughter..."

Philip explains to the Ethiopian that this passage from the Book of Isaiah predicts Jesus dying.

CHAPTER 8 VERSE 39

"... the Spirit of the Lord suddenly took Philip away..."

After baptising the Ethiopian, Philip miraculously vanishes. Amazed at Philip's power, the Ethiopian goes on his way, rejoicing.

ETHIOPIAN'S BAPTISM

As they rode in the chariot, Philip told the Ethiopian that the passage in the book he was reading foretold the coming of Jesus. The Ethiopian was so impressed that, when they reached a pool of water, he asked Philip to baptise him. Philip did as asked, and then he vanished.

Philip baptises the Ethiopian.

The Ethiopian

The New Testament

PAUL

Acts, Chapter 9

A Jew and a Roman citizen, Saul is now better known by his Greek name, Paul. He was a great enemy of the early Church and after hunting down Christians in Jerusalem, he planned to go to Damascus, to see if he could find more to arrest. As Paul and his companions approached Damascus a blinding light came down from heaven. Paul fell to the ground and heard a voice ask, "Why do you persecute me?" Paul asked who was speaking and the voice replied, "I am Jesus, whom you are persecuting".

CHAPTER 9 VERSE 13
"*I have heard many reports about this man...*"
At first Ananias is unwilling to visit Paul. He says he has heard that Paul has come to Damascus to arrest Christians. But Jesus assures Ananias that he has a plan for Paul. Ananias then goes to heal Paul.

CHAPTER 9 VERSE 15
"*This man is my chosen instrument...*"
Jesus tells Ananias that he has given Paul a mission – to preach Christianity to the Gentiles.

PAUL IS BLINDED
After seeing the bright light, Paul was struck blind. His companions, who had not seen the light, helped him to his feet. They led him to Damascus where, for three days, he could not see.

Paul's companion

Paul

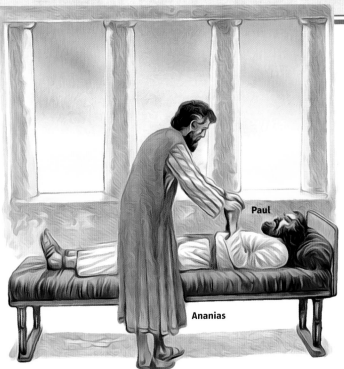

Paul

Ananias

PAUL'S ESCAPE

Paul learned that Jews in Damascus wanted to kill him because of his preachings. He escaped by being lowered from the city wall in a basket. This gate, named Bab Kisan in Damascus, is thought to be the site of his escape. It now houses a chapel dedicated to St Paul.

ANANIAS HEALS PAUL

In Damascus, a disciple called Ananias had a vision in which Jesus told him to go to Paul and restore his sight. Ananias visited Paul, and placed his hands on the blind man, saying that Jesus had sent him. At once, Paul could see again.

PAUL PREACHES

After getting his sight back, Paul became a firm believer in Jesus. In Damascus, Paul went to the synagogues, where the Jews worshipped, and preached that Jesus was the Son of God. Everybody was astonished by the change in Paul.

Paul preaches to the Jews in Damascus.

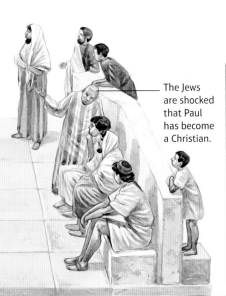

The Jews are shocked that Paul has become a Christian.

HEROD AGRIPPA I

Acts, Chapter 12

Herod Agrippa I, grandson of Herod the Great, was made king of Judea by the Roman Emperor Claudius. To win favour with his Jewish subjects, Herod decided to stop the spread of the Christian religion. First he had the apostle James, brother of John, beheaded with a sword. When this proved popular with the Jewish people, Herod arrested the apostle Peter, planning to put him on trial. Peter was chained, and locked up in a prison cell, which was guarded by soldiers day and night.

HEROD PUNISHES THE GUARDS

Herod was furious when he learned that Peter had escaped. He had the prison searched, and questioned the guards, certain that they had helped Peter escape. He then gave orders for the execution of the guards.

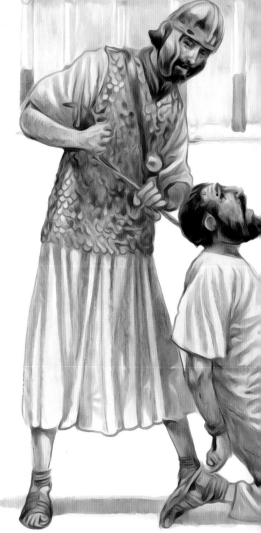

The angel frees Peter.

The guards sleep on.

PETER'S ESCAPE

When Peter was imprisoned, members of the church met to pray. The night before Peter's trial, an angel came to his cell, where he slept between two guards. The angel woke Peter, released him from his chains, and led him to freedom. The church members were amazed at how Peter escaped.

CHAPTER 12 VERSE 23

"... an angel of the Lord struck him down..."

When the people hail Herod as a God, he should have denied it, and praised God. Because he does not, an angel strikes him down.

KING OF JUDEA

Herod Agrippa I grew up in Rome, where he was a friend of the future Emperor Claudius. On becoming emperor, in 41 CE, Claudius made Herod king of Judea. He ruled Judea until his sudden death, just three years later.

Coin from the reign of Herod Agrippa I

Herod is struck down by an angel.

Herod questions one of the guards.

Herod Agrippa I was **the last king of Judea**.

STRUCK DOWN

Later, Herod travelled to the port of Caesarea, where he made a public appearance in a bright silver robe. The crowd praised him by shouting that he was a god rather than a man. When Herod did not deny this, an angel struck him and he was instantly seized with violent pains, and died.

CORNELIUS

Acts, Chapter 10

Cornelius was a Roman centurion who lived in Caesarea, in Judea. Although he was a Gentile (not a Jew), he believed in God. He prayed regularly, and gave generously to the poor. One day, an angel appeared to Cornelius and told him to send soldiers to fetch the apostle Peter, who was staying in Joppa. At the same time, Peter had a vision in which he heard a voice telling him that nothing made by God could be unclean. Many Jews avoided mixing with Gentiles, considering them unclean. Peter understood God's message and willingly agreed to visit Cornelius.

Peter

Cornelius

PETER VISITS CORNELIUS
When Peter reached Cornelius's house, the centurion knelt before him. But Peter asked him to stand up and said, "I am only a man myself." Inside the house, Peter found a crowd gathered to meet him.

CHAPTER 10 VERSE 47
"They have received the Holy Spirit just as we have."
Peter is astonished to see that Gentiles as well as Jews can receive the Holy Spirit. He realizes that Gentiles can be baptised as Christians without becoming Jews first.

Peter watches the Gentiles.

The Gentiles praise God.

THE HOLY SPIRIT
Peter told the Gentiles gathered in the house all about Jesus. At once, they all began to praise God. Peter realized that they had been filled with the Holy Spirit.

JAMES

Acts, Chapter 15

CHAPTER 15 VERSE 29
"You will do well to avoid these things."
In the letter to the Gentiles, James asks them to obey just some basic laws so the Gentiles and Jews could eat together.

James was the brother of Jesus and one of the leading Christians in Jerusalem. He oversaw the very first council (meeting) of the Church held there. This council was held to decide whether Gentiles needed to follow the Law of Moses to be followers of Jesus. Some said that they did want the Gentiles to obey the laws. But Peter, Paul, and Barnabas, who were at the meeting, described the wonders they had seen while preaching to the Gentiles, and James then said that they should help all Gentiles who wanted to be followers of Jesus.

James, also known as **James the Just**, may be the author of the **Epistle of James**.

JAMES SPEAKS
After listening to the other disciples, James suggested that the council should not make life difficult for the Gentiles who had turned to God, by making them follow all the Law of Moses. The council agreed, and sent a letter to the Gentile believers, telling them of their decision.

James

Members of the council listen to James' speech.

PAUL'S JOURNEYS

Acts, Chapters 21–28

SAILING FOR ROME

Paul and some other prisoners were handed over to a Roman officer called Julius. The officer put them on a ship sailing for Rome and they travelled along the southern coastline of Asia Minor (in modern-day Turkey) and then west towards Crete.

The apostle Paul made three missionary journeys around the eastern Mediterranean, founding churches among the Gentiles. When he could not be with his followers in person, he wrote letters offering advice. After his third journey, Paul returned to Jerusalem. His arrival led to a riot, after the Jews there accused him of bringing a Gentile into the temple. Paul was arrested by the Romans and spent two years as a prisoner in Caesarea. He then demanded his right, as a Roman citizen, to be tried by the Emperor in Rome. Paul wanted to go to Rome, so that he could preach there.

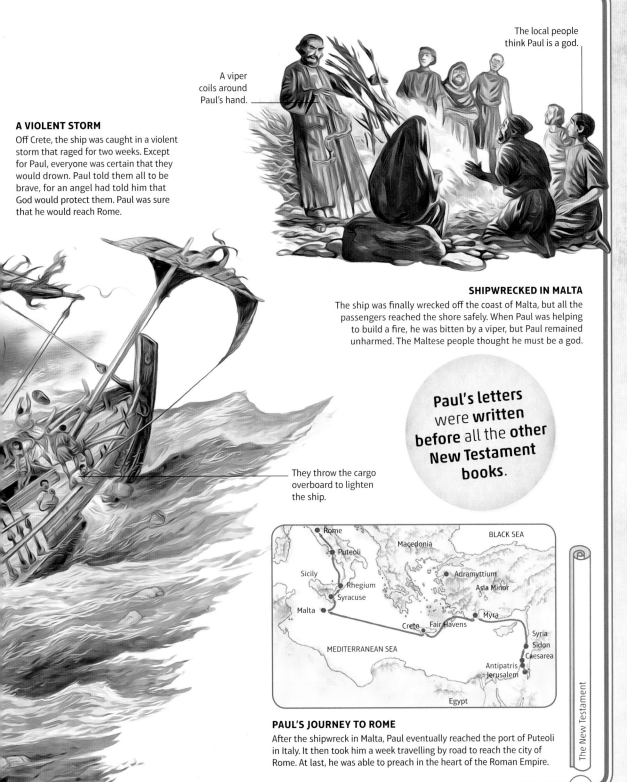

A viper coils around Paul's hand.

The local people think Paul is a god.

A VIOLENT STORM

Off Crete, the ship was caught in a violent storm that raged for two weeks. Except for Paul, everyone was certain that they would drown. Paul told them all to be brave, for an angel had told him that God would protect them. Paul was sure that he would reach Rome.

SHIPWRECKED IN MALTA

The ship was finally wrecked off the coast of Malta, but all the passengers reached the shore safely. When Paul was helping to build a fire, he was bitten by a viper, but Paul remained unharmed. The Maltese people thought he must be a god.

Paul's letters were written before all the other New Testament books.

They throw the cargo overboard to lighten the ship.

Rome
Puteoli
Macedonia
BLACK SEA
Sicily
Adramyttium
Rhegium
Asia Minor
Syracuse
Malta
Myra
Crete Fair Havens
Syria
Sidon
MEDITERRANEAN SEA
Caesarea
Antipatris
Jerusalem
Egypt

PAUL'S JOURNEY TO ROME

After the shipwreck in Malta, Paul eventually reached the port of Puteoli in Italy. It then took him a week travelling by road to reach the city of Rome. At last, he was able to preach in the heart of the Roman Empire.

BARNABAS

Acts, Chapters 4, 9, 11, 13, 15

Barnabas was one of the leaders of the early Church in Jerusalem. He was a Jew from Cyprus and originally known as Joseph. The apostles gave him the name Barnabas, meaning "Son of Encouragement". In Jerusalem, he met Paul (Saul) soon after Paul had become a Christian. Paul told Barnabas how he had seen Jesus on the road to Damascus. Barnabas took Paul to meet the apostles. The apostles were afraid to meet Paul, but Barnabas assured them that Paul was no longer an enemy of the Church. For a while, Barnabas was Paul's travelling companion, until they argued and went their separate ways.

CHAPTER 11 VERSE 26

"The disciples were called Christians first at Antioch."

Before Barnabas and Paul preached in Antioch, followers of Jesus were simply called "believers" or "disciples". The name "Christian" comes from the Greek word meaning "belonging to Christ".

CHAPTER 13 VERSE 46

"... we now turn to the Gentiles."

Paul and Barnabas travel on to Cyprus, where the Jews refuse to listen to their preaching. Paul and Barnabas declare that they will now preach to the Gentiles.

PREACHING IN ANTIOCH

Barnabas and Paul first travelled to Antioch, the capital of Syria. They spent a year in the city, preaching to a great number of people. Though they began by visiting the Jewish synagogues, they had more success winning over the Gentiles (non Jews).

Barnabas tells the people of Antioch about Jesus.

SILAS

Acts, Chapters 15–16

The Gentiles of Antioch welcome Silas.

Judas Barsabbas **Silas**

SILAS DELIVERS JAMES' LETTER

Silas and another church leader, Judas Barsabbas, travelled from Jerusalem to Antioch with James' letter. They delivered it to the Gentiles, who were glad to learn that they did not have to follow the Jewish Law to become Christians.

Silas was a leading member of the Church in Jerusalem. He took part in the first Church council, in which James, the brother of Jesus, decided that Gentiles did not have to obey the Jewish Laws to become Christians. Silas took James' letter, giving this decision, to the Gentiles. After Barnabas and Paul fell out, Paul chose Silas to be his next travelling companion. When they went to Philippi in Macedonia, they were beaten and thrown into prison. During the night, an earthquake broke all the prison doors open, but Paul and Silas stayed in their cell.

CHAPTER 16 VERSE 30

"Sirs, what must I do to be saved?"

Paul and Silas' jailer, astonished by the earthquake that broke open their cell door, asks them how he can be saved. He then converts to Christianity.

CHAPTER 16 VERSE 37

"... we are Roman citizens..."

Paul and Silas are freed after complaining that the authorities had beaten Roman citizens. It was against the law to beat Roman citizens without a trial.

AQUILA AND PRISCILLA

Acts, Chapter 18; **Romans**, Chapter 16

Aquila listens to Paul.

Priscilla

Paul encourages Aquila and Priscilla to preach.

On his second journey, Paul went to Corinth, in Greece. Here Paul met a man called Aquila, and his wife Priscilla, both of whom believed that Jesus was the Messiah. They had left Rome when Emperor Claudius ordered the Jews to leave the city. Like Paul, Aquila and Priscilla were tentmakers. In Corinth, Paul lived with the couple for eighteen months, working with them, both as tentmakers and preachers. Paul got on so well with them that he took them with him when he travelled on to Ephesus (in modern-day Turkey). In his letters, Paul called them his "co-workers in Christ Jesus".

HOUSE CHURCH

The early Church had no special buildings for worship. Instead, Christian believers, such as Aquila and Priscilla, met in small groups in their homes. In one of his letters, Paul passes on his greetings to Aquila and Priscilla, and to "the church that meets at their house".

ACTS
CHAPTER 18 VERSE 2

"... Claudius had ordered all Jews to leave Rome."

The Roman historian Suetonius wrote that Jews, who were followers of "Chrestus", had been driven from Rome for causing disturbances. "Chrestus" was probably Christ.

APOLLOS

Acts, Chapter 18

CHAPTER 18 VERSE 25

"... he knew only the baptism of John."

Apollos knew that baptism was an act that demonstrated repentance, as taught by John the Baptist. But he had not heard about Pentecost, and the gift of the Holy Spirit to the followers of Jesus.

Aquila and Priscilla settled in Ephesus, where they ran a new church from their house. Here they met Apollos, a Jew from Alexandria, Egypt. Apollos had become a Christian, but had heard very little about Jesus Christ. When Aquila and Priscilla heard him preach, they realized that he had not heard of the Holy Spirit. They taught him everything they knew and then encouraged him to travel to Corinth. There Apollos became a leader of the church founded by Paul.

Apollos preaches that Jesus is the Messiah.

PREACHING IN CORINTH

When Apollos reached Corinth, he went to the synagogue, to preach to the Jews who met there. He was a powerful speaker who was well-educated and skilled in argument. Arguing with the Jews, Apollos used the writings of their prophets to prove that Jesus was the promised Messiah.

The Jews of Corinth argue with Apollos.

The New Testament

LUKE

Colossians, Chapter 4; **Acts**, Chapter 28

Luke was a Greek doctor and one of Paul's most faithful companions during his journeys. Paul's final journey ended in Rome where he was kept for two years under house arrest. This meant he could not leave the house, but could receive visitors. Paul's time in Rome was recorded in the Acts of the Apostles, which was written by a companion who travelled there with him. Luke is credited with writing both the Acts and the Gospel of Luke.

COLOSSIANS
CHAPTER 4 VERSE 14

"Our dear friend Luke, the doctor..."

Paul ends his Letter to the Colossians by passing on greetings from Luke, who he describes as a Gentile and a doctor.

ACTS
CHAPTER 28 VERSE 14

"And so we came to Rome."

When describing Paul's difficult journey to Rome, with the shipwreck on Malta, Luke includes himself as a companion. Luke ends the book of Acts with an account of Paul living in Rome.

LUKE VISITS PAUL

While Paul was under house arrest in Rome, we know that Luke visited him from his letters. Paul continued to write letters to his churches throughout his house arrest. In one letter to the church of Colossae (in modern-day Turkey), Paul described himself as a prisoner and sent the Colossians greetings from his companions, which included Luke.

Luke

JOHN MARK

Colossians, Chapter 4; Acts, Chapter 13

COLOSSIANS CHAPTER 4 VERSE 10
"... Mark, the cousin of Barnabas."
In his letter from Rome to the Colossians, Paul passes on greetings from his fellow prisoner, John Mark.

John Mark

Paul

Barnabas

PAUL AND BARNABAS ARGUE

Paul and Barnabas had such a fierce argument about whether John Mark should accompany them on their missionary journey, that they decided to part ways. Barnabas went to Cyprus with John Mark, while Paul went to Syria with Silas. Paul later forgave John Mark, who was with him when he was a prisoner in Rome.

John Mark was the cousin of Barnabas, Paul's companion on his first missionary journey. It was in John Mark's family home that the first Christians met together in Jerusalem. John Mark travelled with Paul and Barnabas to Cyprus, helping them in their mission. When Paul and Barnabas went on to Antioch in Pisidia, he decided not to go with them. Instead, he returned to Jerusalem. This made Paul think he was unreliable. Later, Barnabas told Paul that he wanted to take John Mark with them on their next journey. Paul refused to take him, as John Mark had previously deserted them.

There is a tradition that **John Mark wrote** the **Gospel of Mark**.

3 REFERENCE

THE LAST SUPPER
This mosaic at the Cathedral of Santa Maria Nuova, in Sicily, Italy, shows Jesus and his twelve apostles at their last meal together. In Christian art, the halo (circle of light) around Jesus's head is a sign of holiness.

Find out more about the lands where the stories of the Bible take place. Discover, too, more about other characters in the Bible. A glossary explains the meaning of some of the words used in the book.

LANDS OF THE BIBLE

ITALY
- Rome
- Puteoli

SICILY
- Rhegium
- Syracuse

MALTA

BULGARIA
- Amphipolis
- Philippi
- Thessalonica
- Berea
- Troas
- Adramyttium

GREECE
- Pergamum
- Thyatira
- Antioch in Pisidia
- Smyrna
- Sardis
- Philadelphia
- Corinth
- Athens
- Ephesus
- Laodicea
- Iconium
- Lystra
- Derbe
- Tarsus
- Perga
- Seleucia
- Antioch

PATMOS

CRETE

BLACK SEA

CYPRUS
- Paphos
- Kedes
- Ribla

MEDITERRANEAN SEA

- Damascu
- Sidon

LEBANO

SEA OF GAL

ISRA
- Jericho
- Jerusalem (Jebus)
- Gaza
- **DEAD SE**
- Sodom and Gomorrah
- Pithom
- *NEGEV DESERT*
- Succoti
- Kadesh

EGYPT

SINAI DESERT

- Mt Horeb (Jebel Musa)

River Nile

ETHIOPIA (CUSH)

THE HOLY LAND

- Zarephath
- Mt Hermon
- Tyre
- Caesarea Philippi
- Hazor
- Capernaum
- Cana
- Mt Tabor
- SEA OF GALILEE
- Mt Carmel
- Nazareth
- Shunem
- Megiddo
- Endor
- Jezreel
- Caesarea
- Beth-Shean
- Mt Gilboa
- River Jordan
- River Jabbok
- Samaria
- Shechem
- Succoth
- Joppa
- Shiloh
- Adam
- Ramah (Arimathea)
- Rabbah
- Lydda
- Bethel
- Ai
- Gilgal
- Michmash
- Jericho
- Gibeon
- Gibeah
- Timnah
- Emmaus
- Ekron
- Bethphage
- Bethany
- Ashdod
- Beth Shemesh
- Jerusalem
- Mt Nebo
- Ashkelon
- Gath
- Bethlehem
- Lachish
- Mamre
- Hebron
- Carmel
- Masada
- DEAD SEA
- Beersheba

MEDITERRANEAN SEA

Scale
0	1 in	23 miles
0	25mm	37km

Scale
0	1 inch	150 miles
0	25mm	240km

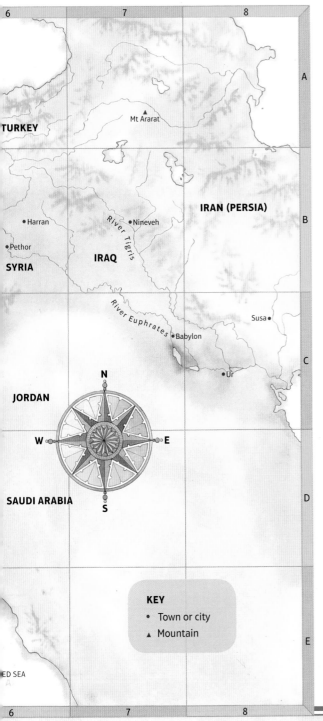

The stories in the Bible are mostly set in the Holy Land – the Promised Land of the Israelites in the Old Testament, and the setting for Jesus's story in the New Testament. Some stories in the Old Testament are set in Egypt and Mesopotamia (modern-day Iraq). The New Testament also follows the journey of Christian preachers across the eastern Mediterranean.

INDEX OF PLACES

The places on the large map are indicated by grid references with upper-case letters and Arabic numerals (eg B2). Places on the inset map are shown with lower-case letters and Roman numerals (eg bii).

MORE BIBLE CHARACTERS

THE OLD TESTAMENT

ABIGAIL
The wife of Nabal, who refused to support the outlawed David by not providing provisions for his army. Abigail managed to persuade David not to punish her husband for this. She later married David.

ACHAN
In the Battle of Jericho, Achan plundered treasures from the fallen city, angering God. Because of this, Joshua's army failed to capture Ai the first time. Joshua had Achan killed for his crime.

ADONIJAH
The fourth son of King David and heir to David's throne. When the throne was given to his brother, Solomon, Adonijah stepped aside.

David
Abigail

Boaz

ARTAXERXES
King of the Persian Empire from 465–424 BCE. He gave his cupbearer, Nehemiah, permission to travel to Jerusalem to start rebuilding the ruined city.

BALAK
King of Moab when the Israelites first entered Canaan. Balak is known for asking the seer (a type of prophet) Balaam to curse his enemy, Israel.

BELSHAZZAR
Descendant of Nebuchadnezzar, he was the co-ruler of Babylon, along with his father, King Nabonidus, from 553–539 BCE. Belshazzar sent for the prophet Daniel when mysterious writing appeared on the palace wall. Daniel told Belshazzar that the writing meant that his kingdom would be conquered by the Persians. Belshazzar was killed that very night by the Persians.

BILHAH
Rachel's servant who was given to Jacob to have children when Rachel could not have any. She gave Jacob two sons.

BOAZ
The wealthy husband of Ruth and King David's great-grandfather. He was from Bethlehem and was a landowner.

CALEB
One of the men sent to spy on the land of Canaan. He was friends with Joshua, and these two were the only adults from the generation who left Egypt to inherit the Promised Land.

DARIUS
The Persian king who conquered Babylon in the time of Daniel. He is known for having Daniel thrown into the lions' den.

ELIMELEK
Husband of Naomi, who died in Moab. He was originally from Bethlehem and had two sons with Naomi.

ELKANAH
The husband of Hannah and the father of the prophet Samuel.

HAGAR
The Egyptian servant of Sarah, Abraham's wife. Hagar was given to Abraham to bear children when Sarah was unable to produce any. Hagar bore Abraham a son called Ishmael, whose descendants were the Ishmaelites.

Hagar

HAGGAI

A prophet from the late 6th century BCE, who wrote the Book of Haggai. He encouraged the Jewish people to complete the rebuilding of the temple in Jerusalem.

HAMAN

A nobleman, favoured by King Xerxes, who plotted to murder all the Jews in the empire. His plans were foiled by Queen Esther and he was killed for his actions.

HANNAH

Married to Elkanah and mother of the prophet Samuel, Hannah prayed to God for a child. When she had Samuel, she was so thankful she dedicated the child to God.

JAEL

Married to Heber the Kenite, Jael is known for killing Sisera, the Commander of the Canaanite army. She lived in the period when the Judges ruled Israel.

JEPHTHAH

A Judge during the 11th century BCE. He saved Israel from the Ammonites.

JOAB

The ruthless commander of King David's army and son of David's sister, Zeruiah, Joab led the army to many victories against the enemies of Israel.

Joab

MANOAH

Father of Israel's mighty warrior, Samson. An angel told Manoah that his son would save Israel from the Philistines.

MICAH

A prophet from the 8th century BCE. His prophecies are written in the Book of Micah.

MORDECAI

Cousin of Queen Esther and a Jew, Mordecai discovered Haman's plot to kill the Jewish people. He reported it to Esther and was promoted to high office.

NAAMAN

A successful warrior and commander of the army of Aram (today in Syria). The prophet Elisha cured Naaman of leprosy.

NABAL

A wealthy man who refused to provide supplies for David's army. David wanted to kill Nabal for this, but Abigail, Nabal's wife, persuaded him not to.

NABOTH

Owner of a vineyard in Jezreel, close to the palace of Ahab, King of Samaria. Ahab wanted the vineyard, but Naboth refused to sell it. Jezebel, Ahab's wife, then spread a rumour that Naboth was blasphemous, and he was put to death.

NIMROD

A Mesopotamian king who founded a kingdom in Babylonia before the time of Abraham. He established many cities, including Babel, and was also a warrior.

RAHAB

An inhabitant of Jericho, Rahab protected the Israelite spies Joshua had sent by hiding them. When Joshua destroyed Jericho, her life was spared and she joined the Israelites.

Naboth

Ahab

SISERA

A commander of the Canaanite army. When Barak and the Israelites defeated his army, Sisera took refuge with Jael, who then killed him.

URIAH

The husband of Bathsheba, sent by David to be killed in a battle against the Ammonites, because Bathsheba was carrying David's child.

XERXES

King of the Persian empire from 486–465 BCE and son of Darius the Great. Xerxes married Esther and made her his queen.

ZILPAH

Leah's servant who was given to Jacob to bear children. She gave him two sons.

THE NEW TESTAMENT

AGABUS

A prophet from Jerusalem who travelled to Antioch, Agabus predicted that Jerusalem's Jewish leaders would capture and hand Paul over to the Gentiles.

ANANIAS

A follower of Jesus who sold some property but kept some of the money for himself, even though the first Christians agreed to share everything they owned.

ANNA

An elderly prophetess from the tribe of Asher, Anna recognized the baby Jesus as the Messiah.

ANNAS

The former High Priest who interrogated Jesus after his arrest.

AUGUSTUS CAESAR

Augustus was the first Roman emperor (31 BCE–14 CE). Jesus was born during his reign.

Simeon

Baby Jesus

Anna

CAIAPHAS

The successor of Annas, Caiaphas was High Priest when Jesus was illegally tried before the Sanhedrin, the chief court of Israel.

Paul

Festus

CLAUDIUS CAESAR

Roman emperor from 41–54 CE, he exiled many Jewish people from Rome in 49 CE because of rioting.

DEMETRIUS

A silversmith who started a riot against Paul in Ephesus. He protested that people had stopped buying silver idols of Artemis, the ancient Greek goddess, because of Paul's preaching.

EPAPHRAS

A companion of Paul, who is mentioned in Paul's letters.

EPAPHRODITUS

One of Paul's companions and a member of the Christian church in Philippi, in Macedonia.

FELIX

A Roman governor, from 52–60 CE, Felix was corrupt and had Paul tried in Caesarea before imprisoning him.

FESTUS

Replacing Felix as governor when he was called back to Rome, Festus was more just and allowed Paul to be lawfully tried in Rome.

GABRIEL

An important angel, Gabriel appeared in the Bible as a messenger from God. Each of his four appearances are associated with the coming of the Messiah.

GALLIO

Roman official of Achaia, who refused to try Paul at a Corinthian court, Gallio was the brother of the Roman philosopher Seneca.

GAMALIEL

A respected Rabbi (a teacher of the Jewish Torah) who stopped the Sanhedrin from putting Peter and the apostles to death.

HEROD AGRIPPA II

Son of Herod Agrippa I, who ruled part of Judea from 50–100 CE. Herod was consulted by the Roman Governor Festus during the trial of Paul.

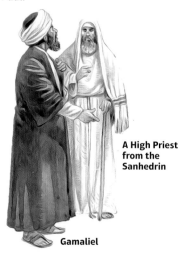

A High Priest from the Sanhedrin

Gamaliel

HERODIAS

The wife of Herod Antipas and the granddaughter of Herod the Great, Herodias is known for her part in the execution of John the Baptist.

JAIRUS

Jairus ruled over the synagogue of Capernaum in Galilee. Jairus asked Jesus to heal his dying daughter. Jesus brought his daughter back from the dead.

Jairus

JOHN OF PATMOS

The author of the Book of Revelation, who lived on Patmos, a Greek island. Some believe him to be John the apostle.

JUDE

Brother of Jesus and traditionally believed to have written the Epistle of Jude.

LYDIA

A Gentile, who was baptized in Philippi by Paul. She was originally attracted to the Jewish traditions but then later became Paul's first Christian convert in Europe.

MARTHA

Sister of Lazarus and Mary (of Bethany), and Jesus's friend.

MARY OF BETHANY

A friend of Jesus and sister of Lazarus and Martha (of Bethany). In Bethany, Mary anointed Jesus's feet with perfume.

MATTHIAS

The man the disciples chose to replace Judas Iscariot after Judas betrayed Jesus and hanged himself in repentance.

ONESIMUS

A former slave of Philemon who had run away to escape punishment. He converted to Christianity after meeting Paul.

PHILEMON

A wealthy Christian who received a letter from Paul, asking him to forgive the former slave Onesimus and receive him back.

SAPPHIRA

Wife of Ananias, she and her husband suddenly died after trying to deceive the Church.

SIMEON

A devout man who recognized baby Jesus as the Messiah when Mary and Joseph brought him to the temple in Jerusalem.

SIMON MAGUS

A sorcerer who tried to buy the Holy Spirit's power from John and Peter.

SIMON OF CYRENE

A visitor from Cyrene who was forced by Roman soldiers to carry the cross when Jesus stumbled under its heavy weight.

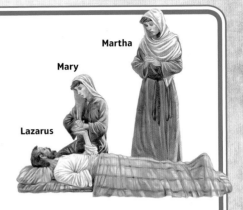

Martha

Mary

Lazarus

TABITHA

Noted for her generosity, Tabitha was an early Christian who was resurrected by Peter after her death.

TERTIUS

Paul's secretary, who wrote down Paul's letter, known as "Romans" in the New Testament.

THE MAN BORN BLIND

A blind man who regained his sight after Jesus healed him. He was questioned by the Pharisees and became a follower of Jesus.

THE PHILIPPIAN JAILER

The prison guard who, upon seeing that Paul and Silas did not escape their jail cell after its doors were opened by an earthquake, became a believer and was baptized.

TIBERIUS CAESAR

During Jesus's ministry, Tiberius was the Roman emperor from 14–37 CE.

TIMOTHY

A missionary and close companion of Paul during his journeys. Paul sent two letters to Timothy.

TITUS

A Greek Christian, Titus was a companion of Paul during his journeys.

GLOSSARY

Altar
A raised table or platform used to make offerings to a god.

Ammonite
The Ammonites were the Israelites' eastern neighbours. According to the Bible, they were descended from Lot's son Ben-Ammi.

Angel
A spiritual being who acts as a servant or messenger of God.

Annunciation
The announcement made by the angel Gabriel to Mary that she would bear the son of God, Jesus Christ.

Anoint
To make holy by applying oil as part of a religious ceremony.

Apostle
One of a group of 12 men who were sent out to spread the teachings of Jesus Christ.

Ark
The large boat built by Noah to save his family, and two of every animal, from a flood sent by God.

Ark of the Covenant
The gold-covered wooden chest holding the two stone tablets of the Ten Commandments.

Assyrian empire
A powerful kingdom that ruled the Middle East from around the 9th to the 7th century BCE.

Baal
A title for a god, rather than the name of a specific god. There were many gods called Baal, including a Canaanite weather god.

Babel
The name of a tower Noah's descendants tried to build, to reach heaven, much against God's will.

Baptism
A Christian ceremony where a person is purified and received into the church community. The person is sprinkled with water or sometimes dipped in water.

BCE/CE
BCE is an abbreviation for Before Common Era. CE is short for Common Era. The Common Era begins with the year 1.

Blasphemy
Words or actions that show disrespect towards God.

Blessing
A solemn speech asking a supernatural power to bestow good on someone or something.

Canaan
The Biblical name of the land between the River Jordan and the Mediterranean. This area now includes Israel and Palestine.

Commandment
A divine rule which, in the Bible, refers to one of the Ten Commandments revealed to Moses.

Covenant
Binding agreement between God and his people.

Crucifixion
A person was bound or nailed to a cross in this ancient form of execution.

Curse
A solemn speech asking a supernatural power to inflict harm on someone or something.

Descendant
Someone who is related to a person or group of people who lived in the past.

Emperor
The supreme ruler of an extensive group of countries or states.

Exodus
The second book of the Bible, which tells of the Israelites' escape from Egypt and the receiving of the Ten Commandments. Also the name of the actual event of the Israelites leaving Egypt.

Galilee
A northern region of ancient Palestine, associated with Jesus's ministry. Today, it is part of Israel.

Genesis
The first book of the Bible in which the story of the world's creation is told.

Gentile
A person who is not Jewish.

Gospel
The message and teachings of Jesus Christ. Also the name of the four New Testament books describing his life.

Hebrew
A name originally given to Abraham and his family, whose later descendants were called Israelites and Jews. Also the name of the Jewish language.

High Priest
The chief priest of the Jewish religion in Biblical times.

Holy Spirit
The spirit of God. For Christians, the Holy Spirit is one of the three persons, or forms, of God, along with the Father and the Son (Jesus Christ).

Idol
An image of a god used as an object of worship.

Israel and Judah
According to the Bible, when Rehoboam succeeded his father Solomon, in about 930 BCE, the country split into two kingdoms: Israel in the north and Judah in the south. Judah is also known as Judea, which is its later Roman name.

Israelite
A member of the ancient Hebrew nation, especially from the 13th century BCE to the 6th century BCE.

Jew
A person who traces their family line back to the Hebrew people of Israel. The traditional religion of the Jews is called Judaism.

Judge
Name given to the leaders of the Israelite tribes in the period starting at the end of Joshua's leadership and finishing before the reign of the first King of Israel, Saul.

Mesopotamia
The ancient region in present-day Iraq, located between the Rivers Tigris and Euphrates. Its plains were the sites of the civilizations of Assyria, Babylonia, Sumer, and Akkad.

Miracle
An event that cannot be explained by the known laws of nature, and is thought to be caused by divine power.

Pagan
A name given by Christians to people who worshipped other gods.

Philistine
The name of the people of ancient southern Palestine who came into conflict with the Israelites roughly during the 11th and 12th centuries BCE.

Prayer
An expression of thanks or a solemn request made to God.

Promised Land
The land of Canaan promised by God to Abraham and his descendants in the Old Testament.

Prophecy
A prediction of future events, and a message from God given by a prophet.

Prophet
A person seen as an inspired proclaimer or teacher of God's will.

Province
Name given to one of the divisions of the Roman Empire. Each province had its own governor.

Resurrection
Coming back to life after death, especially Jesus's return to life after his crucifixion.

Sacrifice
An act of surrendering a possession, or killing an animal or person, as an offering to God.

Saviour
Someone who saves someone from peril. In Christianity, the Saviour is Jesus Christ, who saves people's souls from punishment after death.

Scripture
The sacred writings of Christianity contained in the Bible.

Sin
An act seen as a regrettable or serious offence, fault, or omission in the eyes of God.

Tabernacle
A tent used by the Israelites as a place of worship during the Exodus and the time of the Judges.

Transfiguration
A Biblical term to describe Jesus's temporary appearance as a heavenly being.

Tribe
A distinctive or close-knit group of people who live together.

Worship
Religious rites or ceremonies in which a person formally shows their love and respect for a god.

INDEX

ACKNOWLEDGMENTS

Dorling Kindersley would like to thank the following people for their assistance with this book:
Antara Moitra, Rupa Rao, and Deeksha Saikia for editorial assistance; Anna Limerick and Ann Baggaley for proofreading, and Carron Brown for the index.

Picture Credits

The publisher would like to thank the following for their kind permission to reproduce their photographs:

(Key: a–above; b–below/bottom; c–centre; f–far; l–left; r–right; t–top)

8 akg–images: Erich Lessing (cl). **Alamy Stock Photo:** ART Collection (crb); Ira Berger (ca); www.BibleLandPictures.com (cl/scroll). **9 akg–images:** Pictures From History (cl); Bildarchiv Steffens (clb). **Getty Images:** Mondadori Portfolio (cr). **10 Getty Images:** Stefano Bianchetti (cra); Fred De Noyelle / GODONG (clb). **10–11 123RF.com:** Jozef Sedmak (b). **11 Alamy Stock Photo:** Heritage Image Partnership Ltd (cr); Science History Images (cla). **Getty Images:** ZU_09 (cra). **12–13 akg–images:** Erich Lessing. **14 Alamy Stock Photo:** www.BibleLandPictures.com (cl). **14–15 Alamy Stock Photo:** Lebrecht Music and Arts Photo Library (c). **15 Bridgeman Images:** French School / Museo Nazionale del Bargello, Florence, Italy (cla); Look and Learn (cra). **Getty Images:** Heritage Images (c); Roger Ressmeyer / Corbis / VCG (cb). **25 Dreamstime.com:** Gurkan Ozturk (crb). **27 Dreamstime.com:** Michael Klenetsky (tr). **29 Depositphotos Inc:** Homocosmicos (crb). **39 Alamy Stock Photo:** Pauline Thornton (ca). **41 Alamy Stock Photo:** Everett Collection Inc (cra). **43 Alamy Stock Photo:** Claudia Wiens (cra). **49 Getty Images:** Werner Forman (crb). **51 Getty Images:** Stefano Ravera (ca). **57 Getty Images:** ALESSANDRO VANNINI (crb). **61 123RF.com:** Robert Hoetink (crb). **63 Alamy Stock Photo:** Duby Tal (cr). **65 Alamy Stock Photo:** Granger Historical Picture Archive (cra). **67 Dreamstime.com:** James Williams (crb). **75 Alamy Stock Photo:** Walker Art Library (cb). **81 Alamy Stock Photo:** Danita Delimont (cra). **83 Dreamstime.com:** James Steidl (cra). **97 Bridgeman Images:** Private Collection / Peter Willi (ca). **103 iStockphoto.com:** Shane Gross (cra). **113 Alamy Stock Photo:** imageBROKER (crb). **118–119 Getty Images:** Print Collector. **120 Alamy Stock Photo:** Art Reserve (cra). **120–121 Bridgeman Images:** Bonhams, London, UK (b). **121 akg–images:** Pictures From History (cla). **Alamy Stock Photo:** Robert Harding (crb). **Dorling Kindersley:** Jamie Marshall (cra).

127 Alamy Stock Photo: INTERFOTO (cra). **129 Getty Images:** ALESSANDRO VANNINI (cra). **133 Dreamstime.com:** Witr (crb). **134 Dreamstime.com:** Jdazuelos (ca). **137 Alamy Stock Photo:** Peter Horree (ca). **139 Alamy Stock Photo:** Itsik Marom (ca). **145 Alamy Stock Photo:** Beniamin Gelman (crb). **147 Alamy Stock Photo:** Lanmas (cra). **151 Alamy Stock Photo:** www.BibleLandPictures.com (crb). **153 Getty Images:** DEA / G. DAGLI ORTI (ca). **155 akg–images:** Erich Lessing (cra). **159 Alamy Stock Photo:** Duby Tal / Albatross (cra). **161 Alamy Stock Photo:** www.BibleLandPictures.com (cra). **163 Getty Images:** DEA / A. DAGLI ORTI (cra). **165 Alamy Stock Photo:** Israel images (crb). **167 Getty Images:** Richard Fairless (cra). **171 Alamy Stock Photo:** Chris Willemsen (cr). **173 Alamy Stock Photo:** PS–I (cra). **175 Alamy Stock Photo:** Raj Singh (cra). **179 Alamy Stock Photo:** Sonia Halliday Photo Library (cra). **181 Alamy Stock Photo:** imageBROKER (cra). **183 Alamy Stock Photo:** dbimages (cra). **185 Alamy Stock Photo:** www.BibleLandPictures.com (cra). **196–197 Alamy Stock Photo:** imageBROKER.

All other images © Dorling Kindersley
For further information see:
www.dkimages.com